Ash tree, *Fraxinus excelsior*, in a hedgerow, Stour Valley, Dorset.

In memory of

The Ash Tree

OLIVER RACKHAM

A LITTLE TOLLER **MONOGRAPH**

Published by Little Toller Books in 2014

Little Toller Books, Lower Dairy, Toller Fratrum, Dorset

Typeset in Garamond Monotype and Perpetua by Little Toller Books

Printed by TJ International, Padstow, Cornwall

All papers used by Little Toller Books are natural, recyclable products made from wood grown in sustainable, well-managed forests

A catalogue record for this book is available from the British Library

ISBN 978-1-908213-14-3

Contents

Fig. 1 A field ash in West Stafford, Dorset.

Preface

ASH IS ONE OF THE COMMONEST TREES, from the mountains of South Wales to the glens of Scotland, the hedges of Ireland, and the railway banks of the English Midlands. Most ash trees are wildlife, like bluebells or badgers or birch trees; they look after themselves and cost nothing. Ash is under-appreciated: it has not the glamour of birch, the mystery of lime, the ruggedness of black poplar, the antiquity of yew, the magic of rowan, or the lore and legend of oak. It is a very recognisable tree that people are fond of in a quiet way, but not one that people are moved to write books about.

There are nearly as many ash trees in Britain as there are people – but what does such a statement mean? Like most statistics, it is hedged about with problems of definition (how big does a little ash tree have to get before it is counted?). The internet has plenty of official figures about ash, but not knowing exactly what they mean I shall not make much use of them.

Everyone knows what an ash tree looks like. There is only one British species. Ash comes into leaf late and loses its leaves early. In summer the compound leaves (with leaflets on either side of a midrib and one leaflet at the end) in opposite pairs are highly distinctive. In autumn the leaves fall usually while still green, but may turn yellow; the bunches of flattened ash *keys*, each one enclosing a seed, then fall (*see* Fig. 5, page 15). In winter it is recognised by the thick curving twigs in opposite pairs, with fat dull-black buds. Ash bark is pale grey, but now increasingly covered with many-coloured lichens. The tree spreads widely where it has room: most old ashes have several trunks from a common base (Fig. 2). It can be a huge tree, second only to lime as the tallest of native trees. It is one of the few trees to have a distinctive sound – the clattering of the twigs of an ashwood in a gale is unforgettable.

I was asked to write this book as a response to the first noticing of 'Ash Dieback' disease in Britain in 2012. This was seized on by the Press as a man-made disaster and a scandal that should have been avoided. Ash is a successful tree that is more than capable of taking care of itself: yet people had been planting ash trees in their millions, and importing little ash trees by the million, and inevitably introducing this inconspicuous pathogen, which supposedly was on the way to killing every ash tree in Europe.

As I shall show, on present information it would be wrong to put all the blame for Ash Disease on the nursery trade. But the disease was not an isolated event: it brought to immediate public attention something that I have been rabbiting on about for years without anyone listening. The greatest threat to the world's trees and forests is globalisation of plant diseases: the casual way in which plants and soil are shipped and flown around the globe in commercial quantities, inevitably bringing with them diseases to which the plants at their destination have no resistance. This has been subtracting

Fig. 2 Big ash stool in Buff Wood, Cambridgeshire. Multiple stems show it has been felled many times; the last time was in 1936.

Fig. 3 Ash hedge in Dorset, no longer maintained. The horizontal stems were *plashed* or *laid* in the past, after which their branches grew vertically.

tree after tree from the world's ecosystems: if it goes on for another hundred years how much will be left?

Oak and hazel, like ash, once looked after themselves and cost nothing, but they now have lost much of their power to grow from seed – oak perhaps from the introduction of the oak mildew fungus, hazel from the deliberate introduction of the grey squirrel. Before the latest round of Elm Disease, elms used to be in this category too. Ash is the commonest remaining self-maintained tree, followed by birch. Some trees should continue to be wildlife, retaining their independence from the human species: partly because people's enthusiasm for trees comes and goes on a shorter timescale than the lifespan of trees; but also because *Homo sapiens* has proved to be an increasingly unreliable guardian of the world's trees.

Acknowledgements

This book is a by-product of a lifetime's interest in ash and other trees. I acknowledge my debt to early friends and colleagues, including (among many others) David Coombe, Peter Grubb, Colin and Susan Ranson, and James and Ann Hart. Recently I have had much help from Nigel Spring, Peter Fordham, Simon Leatherdale, Peter Austin, Tomasz Wazny, Valerie Cooper, Mark Powell, Mark Hill, Paula Keen, Rigas Tsakiris and Jennifer Moody. Louise Bacon has helped me to much useful material on ash lichens and Ash Disease. Gary Battell, expert on tree diseases and many other things, has been a great help on gathering material for this book.

Fig. 4 Giant woodland ash tree in Wytham Woods, Oxford, 2013.

1 The ash tree: what it is and how it behaves

> So much, then, for the ash, a tree which has divided the opinions, perhaps of more writers than any other similar object; for whilst some have gravely told us that it should never be allowed to appear near a dwelling, others have discerned in it a very graceful character, and have termed it the "Venus of the Woods."
>
> GRIGOR, *Eastern Arboretum*

ASH IS NEARLY UBIQUITOUS in Britain and Ireland. *The New Atlas of the British and Irish Flora* shows it as 'native' in almost every 10-km square except in the north-west fringes of Ireland, two tracts in the central and northern Highlands of Scotland, most of Caithness and most of the Hebrides. It is not native in Orkney, Shetland, and (in my opinion) the Isles of Scilly. Its fringe distribution may have retreated, for on the edges there are squares with only pre-1970 records. I suspect, however, that its native distribution has been exaggerated: in much of The Fens, with no native woodland, ash is probably only an introduction, put there by someone.

Ash tolerates many climates and soils. It is said to go up to 450 m (1,480 feet) in the mountains of South Wales. Although it leafs late, it suffers temporary damage from late frost.

Ash grows all over north and middle Europe, stopping well short of the Arctic Circle. In southern Europe and in Asia other species of ash replace it.

Reproduction

> Have you ever looked at the common Ash? I find in my Field 3
> classes of Trees; viz (1) females (seed-producers with aborted
> anthers, & rarely with a single good anther (2) Hermaphrodite
> (seed-producers) in my field few in number (3) Males 'bristling'
> with good-sized pistils [female parts] & stigmas, which soon
> drop off & with atrophied ovules: these male trees *apparently* do
> not produce a single seed . . .
>
> Letter from Charles Darwin to J.D. Hooker, 23 April, 1863

Ash is not a clonal tree, growing from suckers like aspen
or most elms. It normally reproduces by seed. The flowers,
opening just before the leaves in mid spring, can be male
or female or bisexual. The densely clustered flowers are
as simple as flowers can be: each consists of two stamens
and/or an ovary, without petals or sepals, and producing no
nectar[1].

Whole trees tend towards one sex or the other, but this
is not clear-cut and may change from year to year. Ash is
pollinated by both wind and insects (for a few days it yields
pollen for hive-bees). Pollen analysts reckon it to be a sparse
producer of pollen, under-represented in finds of prehistoric
pollen. Like oak and beech, it fruits heavily only in some
years, such as 2013.

The male tree was said to have denser foliage than the
female; John Loudon, the nineteenth-century arboricultural
writer, recommends that ornamental planters go to the
trouble of grafting their ash trees to make sure they are male.

The dry winged keys of ash, belonging to the class of

1 *Fraxinus ornus*, the common ash of southern Europe, has
'normal' flowers with sepals and petals.

Fig. 5 Ash from Jan Kops's *Flora Batava* published in 1800, showing the compound leaves and the fruits or 'keys' that ripen in September (1); the buds opening in April (2); female, hermaphrodite and male flowers (3); and (4) the fully opened flower clusters.

fruits called *samaras*, are blown away by wind for 200 yards or more: thus ash spreads and takes over newly available ground. Whether animals also carry the seeds is less well known.

Ash seed usually waits a year before it germinates and sets out on the long and hazardous stages of becoming a tree. (If every ash seed turned into a tree, in two generations the world would not be big enough to hold them.) It has been said that ash is light-demanding, avoiding shade, an early

Fig. 6 Suppressed ashling. Although only a foot or so high, it is many years old, having struggled against shade and browsing animals. Each kink represents where an animal has bitten the top off after a year's growth. If it gets away to form a tree, it will retain a gnarled base for many years.

successional tree, occupying the ground for one generation before being replaced by 'climax' trees like oak. If ever this were true it is no longer. Oak is now light-demanding: young oak trees are abundant in heaths, railway land, abandoned fields, anywhere except in an existing wood. Ash is relatively shade-tolerant. If nothing eats it in its first year, an ashling can survive for many years in moderate shade as a dwarfed, bonsai-like tree; it even survives occasional browsing by deer (Fig. 6). As soon as a canopy gap appears, for example by the fall of a single oak, a group of ashlings will struggle up towards the light. For many years they retain a gnarled base as witness to their early suppression or to deer attack (Fig. 7).

Ash seedlings compete poorly with vigorous dog's mercury, which often forms a dense, nearly evergreen canopy

Fig. 7 Pole-size ashes with gnarled bases, Hayley Wood, Cambridgeshire.

some 10 inches high. It can influence the tree composition of woods by excluding new ash trees, which are killed by damping-off fungi before they overtop the mercury.

Coppicing and pollarding

If cut down an ash tree sprouts from the stump, even at a quite advanced age. Dormant buds under the bark, vestiges of the bases of leaves and twigs shed years ago, are stimulated into growth and bore their way out through the bark, which sometimes takes more than a year. New shoots (if deer leave

Fig. 8 Ancient ash stools still function, after at least 500 years, producing crops of poles. Bradfield Woods, in March (*above*) and June (*below*) 1981.

them alone) grow 3–4 feet in the first year, occasionally much more (Fig. 10 and Fig. 12). Since prehistoric times people have known that the resulting poles are more useful than the big tree.

In most woods it has been the custom (for unknown reasons) to cut ash at 2–3 feet above ground, rather than at ground level. Ash thus forms a *stool* above ground, which goes on sprouting indefinitely; it gets bigger in diameter each time round (Fig. 8).

If the tree is pollarded – cut several feet above ground – it sprouts all the way up (Fig. 9), but animals usually eat the new shoots as high as they can reach, forming a *browse-line*. Stems produced by coppiced or pollarded trees are called *wood*, in contrast to *timber* from felling trees big enough to make beams and planks.

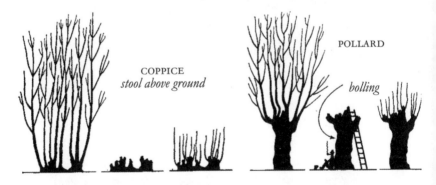

COPPICE
stool above ground

POLLARD

bolling

Fig. 9 Coppicing and pollarding of ash. The tree is shown before cutting, after cutting, and one year after cutting.

Fig. 10 Coppice growth of ash within one season after felling. This is exceptional: average growth (even without deer) would be no more than half this. Chalkney Wood, Essex.

Timber and wood

Ash is a *ring-porous* tree. When the leaves come out it begins to lay down the year's new wood, starting with one or two rows of big *vessels*, the tubes that move sap up the tree. As the season continues it lays down more compact wood in which smaller vessels are embedded. In a cross-section of a stem the annual rings are very conspicuous, the big vessels being just visible to the naked eye.

Ash timber and wood have four useful properties. They

are 'tough', resilient and shock-resistant. They are kind to human hands, not producing sharp 'shivers' like oak and pine, and can be used for heavy-duty handles. They can be steam-bent. They do not taint food and drink as oak, elm, and pine do.

Ash is hard and can be heavy: reference tables give it a specific gravity of around 0.7 (700 kg per cubic metre, 44 pounds per cubic foot), referring presumably to the air-dry weight. Like oak and other ring-porous woods, ash is lighter and weaker when slow-grown. I found specimens of fast-grown ash pollard wood to have a specific gravity of 0.88 when fresh, 0.68 when air-dry. Loudon gives ash a specific gravity of 1.03 when fresh (it would sink in water) and 0.79 when dry: evidently an exceptionally dense and fast-grown specimen.

The pink colour of newly-felled ash soon fades through orange to nearly white. Ash has a distinct heartwood, darker in colour than the sapwood. The heartwood often turns black, which is regarded as a defect (unlike in other black-hearted trees), although it seems not to weaken the timber.

Ash can be steamed: it bends easily when heated to 100°C and sets into a rigid shape as it cools. Many trades involve splitting ash, holding a pole in a kind of vice called a *brake* and cleaving it with an iron tool called a *froe*. I find ash more difficult to cleave in a controlled manner than oak or hazel.

Ash rots quickly: ash posts in a deer fence in Hayley Wood, Cambridgeshire, lasted only four to five years, although a structure with earth-fast ash posts in Bradfield Woods, Suffolk, has lasted 20 years. Cleft ash poles are used as horizontal rails in fences where the posts that go in the ground are oak.

The width of individual annual rings is related to the weather. In Hayley Wood near Cambridge good years, e.g. 1903, 1912, 1924, 1936, 1950, 1958, tend to go with wet summers. The exceptionally dry summers of 1975–6 are marked by narrow rings in most ash trees in this and other woods, although other bad years, such as 1915 and 1930, appear to correspond to summer drought in the *previous* year. It should be possible to set up a *dendrochronology* for ash (Fig. 11), enabling historic artefacts to be dated from ring-width patterns, as has been done for oak, but so far there is not enough historic material.

Longevity

Trees do not have a well-defined term of life like the 'threescore and ten' of humanity. Unlike the human species, a tree enlarges every year: its lifespan is limited by a growing imbalance between supply and demand for the material produced by the leaves. Most trees reach nearly their maximum height and spread comparatively young. Thereafter, averaging good and bad years, a tree produces roughly the same amount of substance annually. This substance is laid down as a new annual ring of wood over an inexorably increasing surface area of twigs, branches, trunk, and roots. The time comes when this is unsustainable.

Trees can delay the ageing process by abandoning twigs, branches and roots that no longer 'pay their way'. Some forms of dieback, like that of ash in 1975–6 (*see* p.140), although regarded as drought adaptation or attributed to disease, may have the effect of re-setting the clock and re-establishing

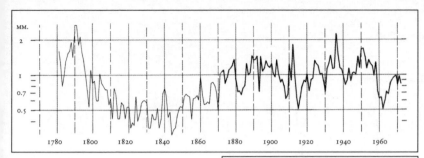

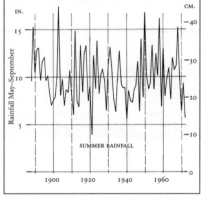

Fig. 11 Mean widths of annual rings of ash (based on 18 trees) compared with rainfall from May to September inclusive, Hayley Wood, Cambridgeshire. Rainfall is recorded in Cambridge, where records do not go back beyond 1888 (they seldom do), but the last phase of the Little Ice Age is a possible explanation for slow growth after 1810.

a balance between supply and demand. In a forest a tree is forever competing with its neighbours, and as soon as it dies back it loses its space to another tree. An isolated tree has the opportunity to retrench and grow back. Hence the longest lived trees of a species tend not to be in forests but free-standing individuals. With many trees, the oldest individuals are those that grow in adverse environments, such as high mountains where the growing season is short and the clock ticks slowly; fast-growing individuals in optimum environments seldom live long.

With ash, longevity is promoted by woodcutting. Every

Fig. 12 Ash hedge two years after being plashed ('laid'). This contains only a few individual ash trees and, as shown by the thicker horizontal stems, has been plashed many times. Toller Fratrum, Dorset, 2014.

time a tree is pollarded or coppiced the clock is reset. An ash tree in a favourable environment, if not cut down, usually falls to pieces and disappears at about 200 years. If periodically cut down (coppiced or pollarded) it regrows indefinitely, and will often live to 400 or more.

Ash and animals

Ash does not seem to be associated with many beasts and birds. The young shoots are very palatable to cattle, sheep and deer – deer are the second major threat to the future of ash trees. I spent an instructive afternoon watching the Indian elephants of Whipsnade Zoo meet the various hedgerow trees of the farm that had preceded the zoo. They were fond of oak bark, scraping it with their toenails and prising with their tusks. They ate whitebeam bark and hawthorn twigs; they also fed on hornbeam faggots. The elephants, however, would not touch ash.

I shall not list every bird that has ever sat on an ash tree. Ash trees (and aspen) are particularly good for hole-nesting birds. Woodpeckers like to bore nest holes into rotten ashes, and these holes are reused by other birds. Bats use particular parts and stages of veteran ashes for roosting and breeding sites, as they do other trees. Ash bark is much eaten by hares and rabbits in winter, but rarely by grey squirrels. As far as I know people never feed on ash, even if they have nothing else to eat (but *see* 'Uses of ash leaves', p. 101).

According to the database of the Biological Records Centre, ash is the food-plant of 111 species of insects and mites. Of these, 29 are specific to ash (or to ash and its specific fungus *Daldinia*) among native trees. A further 6 are common to ash and wild privet (another member of the Oleaceæ).

There is no ash butterfly to correspond with the White-Letter Hairstreak which feeds solely on elm. Among moths, the Centre-Barred Sallow, *Atethmia centrago*, despite its name, is an ash feeder. The Dusky Thorn, *Ennomos fuscantaria*, feeds on ash and privet (and on the exotic horsechestnut). Three micro-moths are ash feeders, and one on ash and privet.

Ash thus has a modest number of insect feeders, although this may increase as veteran trees (*see* p.64) become better known. Oak (*Quercus robur*) in the same database has 275 insect and mite feeders: this cannot be wholly due to a greater intensity of recording, for oak has 35 species of *Andricus*, the little wasps that produce a huge variety of galls only on oak, whereas ash has not one. Hazel has 252; beech has 200; whereas lime (*Tilia cordata*) has only 37. (Is it a coincidence that ash and lime are glomero-mycorrhizal and have correspondingly few associated toadstools?).

Ash lichens

> The elephant-grey bark begins to gleam in a light rain shower.
> I love this skin of ash, almost human in its perfect smoothness
> when young, with an under-glow of green.
>
> Roger Deakin, *Wildwood* (written 2005–6)

Lichens are not parasites: they grow on trees as a support, much as lichens do on rocks, not deriving their sustenance from the tree. Some lichens grow on twigs, others on the trunk or big branches. Lichens also grow on bare wood, though not much on ash wood because it soon rots. For some lichens the species of tree matters; other lichens grow on both rocks and trees.

Deakin's description is not of ash bark in its 'natural' state, but of ashes whose lichen cover has been impoverished by air pollution. There have been two historic changes in lichen floras. In the industrial period, acid rain – mainly sulphuric acid from burning coal – killed most of the lichens in, or downwind of, cities and areas of industry. This reached its peak in the 1960s as high-sulphur oil replaced coal for domestic heating. Since then, acid rain has largely been replaced by pollution from atmospheric nitrogen compounds,

Fig. 13 Twigs and small branches, especially of ash, are now covered in lichens as they were not 20 to 40 years ago, before the decline of acid rain. Hatfield Forest, Essex, May 2009.

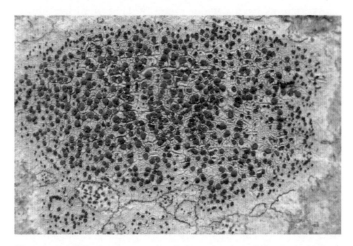

Fig. 14 *Lecidella elaiochroma*, one of the commoner lichens on the bark of small ash trunks. Great Glemham, Suffolk, August 2013.

derived from motor engines, the front and back ends of dairy cattle, and fertiliser dust. In remote, mainly western, areas such as Kingcombe, Dorset, something approximating to the pre-industrial lichen flora still exists. In much of the country the lichen flora is dominated by species that tolerate, indeed require, pollution by nitrogen compounds. In a few areas lichens are still restricted to those few species that tolerate acid rain.

Twig lichens respond rapidly to these changes. Ash twigs are now typically grey and yellow (which they were not in the 1980s) with nitrophilous lichens, mostly a few common species of *Xanthoria*, *Physcia*, and *Lecanora* (Fig. 13). These flourish on ash, with its weakly acid bark, light shade and short leafing season. In areas that have never had acid rain, oak is probably richer than ash in twig lichens.

Ash trunks have a wider range of lichens, especially the rugged bark of big, old, unshaded trees. Trunk lichens are less responsive to environmental change: the alkaline bark gives some resistance to acid rain, but takes longer to recover. Ash has fewer species dependent on *old* trees than oak.

According to the British Lichen Society, about 600 species of lichens, more than a quarter of the total flora, have been recorded on ash. Does this reflect more than the ubiquity of ash trees? Most of them occur also on other trees, especially with moderately alkaline bark, such as elm and sycamore. Only two lichens, *Lithothelium phæosporum* and *Thelenella modesta*, are known only from ash, the latter being confined to just one tree. Several others are mainly on ash, especially on ash trees in the hyper-oceanic climate of Atlantic hazelwoods. Ash is a last refuge of declining tree lichens, especially those that used to grow also on big elms – big elms that have survived Elm Disease, except on the Isles of Scilly, are mostly in areas that lost their lichens to acid rain.

Ash fungi

All trees, indeed most land plants, need to have certain fungi attached to their roots to grow properly. Such *mycorrhizal* fungi spread out into the soil as a 'wood-wide web' of microscopic threads that greatly increase the root's efficiency: they derive their substance from the tree and supply the tree with water and minerals from the soil. Most trees have fungi that form

Fig. 15 The wood-rotting bracket *Inonotus hispidus*: a common polypore with a large, dark-coloured bracket and a conspicuously hairy upper surface, sprouting from injury sites especially on ash. It is often associated with breakage of ash.

Fig. 16 Two of the many wood-rotting fungi that grow on ash, among other trees: *Crepidotus variabilis* on twig (*above*) and *Coryne sarcoides* on a small mossy stump (*below*).

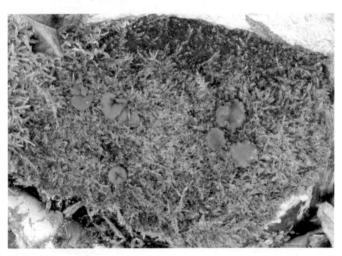

conspicuous toadstools: for example, the famous fly-agaric is found only under birch and pine. Ash, lime and hawthorn, however, along with grasses and most herbaceous plants, are associated with specialised fungi called Glomeromycetes: these are inconspicuous and are never seen except by those mycologists who specialise in studying them. These *glomalean* mycorrhizas are the older of the two kinds, going back to the Palæozoic origin of land plants.

Thus there are few toadstools specifically associated with ash and lime, compared with many under oak, beech, or hazel. Ash has few litter-decomposing fungi, for its fallen leaves are attractive to earthworms and are dragged into their burrows and eaten below ground. Only where ash grows in soils too acid or too wet to have worms do the leaves pile up to be consumed by fungi.

Ash, however, has its share of wood-rotting fungi, some specific to ash. The most familiar is *Daldinia concentrica*, which some wit nicknamed King Alfred's Cakes, the spherical, black, charcoal-like excrescences that are common on dead ash wood. A number of beetles live only on this fungus and are dependent – in Britain – on ash. Another ash fungus is the wood-rotting bracket *Inonotus hispidus* (Fig. 15).

Ash mosses and liverworts

Ash is a substrate for many mosses and liverworts, particularly on the rugged bases of veteran coppice stools and on the bigger trunks of overstood coppice ash. Ash is more prolific than oak and less than elder. In Lowland England, ash trees have a similar bryophyte flora to maple; in the north and west ash resembles sycamore.

Among the richest woods are the Atlantic hazelwoods of the coastal fringes of western Scotland and Ireland. These sometimes contain old stools of ash, which like the hazels are dripping with mosses and liverworts.

There are 26 mosses and 4 liverworts particularly associated with ash, although none is confined to it. In Lowland England ash and maple are the main habitat of three mosses, *Isothecium alopecuroides*, *Homalia trichomanoides* and *Neckera complanata*. Others, such as *Orthotrichum* species, that used to be confined to ash, have increased with the decline of acid rain and now grow on other trees as well. What may be a recent change is the growth of a 'sock' of common bark-mosses on the bottom foot or so of small suppressed ash trees in woods (Fig. 22).

In 1967 Jeff Duckett, bryologist, found the then rare liverwort *Lejeunea cavifolia* on a stool base of ash in Hayley Wood, Cambridgeshire. I marked the tree; 41 years later, Professor Duckett returned to the wood and we refound *Lejeunea* on the selfsame tree: it was still a single patch no bigger than a teacup.

Storms

As the great storms of 1987 and 1990 showed, ash uproots less easily than most trees. As far as I can tell, like most British trees, it has no tap-root (Fig. 17). Like other trees it survives uprooting if one-sixth of the roots remains in the ground; if not too shaded by neighbouring trees it comes to terms with the new direction of gravity and grows new stems from the prostrate trunk.

Ashes do not break easily in storms, with one exception:

Fig. 17 Uprooted ash tree. The shallow rooting depth is typical for ash in boulder-clay woods. A wind-blown ash with this amount of root left in the ground would usually stay alive; this tree, however, probably fell because the fungus *Pholiota squarrosa* had damaged its roots. Hatfield Forest, Essex, May 2009.

Fig. 18 Tall, youngish ash tree that collapsed at two narrow forks, on different occasions. Madingley Wood, Cambridgeshire, 2007.

narrow forks (Fig. 18) split apart. These are not primarily due
to fungal attack but are probably genetic. If something eats
or kills the terminal bud of a young tree, the two opposite
buds below may take over and form a pair of new leading
shoots. If the fork is wide, as the leaders get thicker the bark
is pushed out of the way and the fork remains stable. With a
narrow fork, a fold of bark is trapped and forms a permanent
weakness. Many years later, one half of the fork splits off in
a storm and crashes down. In the next storm the other half
crashes down in the opposite direction.

Garden varieties of ash

There are many cultivars of ash, probably more fashionable in
the nineteenth century than now. The best known is weeping
ash, which Loudon said in 1838 had been 'discovered, about

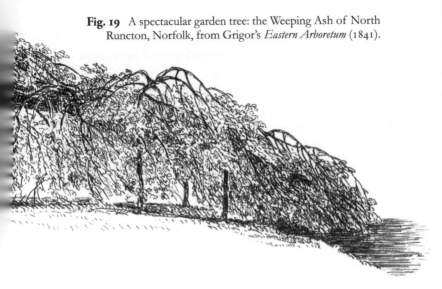

Fig. 19 A spectacular garden tree: the Weeping Ash of North Runcton, Norfolk, from Grigor's *Eastern Arboretum* (1841).

the middle of the last century, in a field belonging to the vicar of Gamlingay' in Cambridgeshire. The vicar had enlarged his garden to include the tree, which in Loudon's time had become 'comparatively in ruins'. Weeping ash is grafted at the top of an ordinary ash tree and grows downwards; it can be spectacular.

Ashwoods

Along with oak, birch, beech and hazel, ash is one of the chief woodland trees of England, and to a lesser extent of Wales, Scotland and Ireland, and has been steadily getting commoner. It is unusual for a wood, unless a plantation, to be entirely of ash. But nearly all woods have some ash trees (even Merthen Wood in far west Cornwall, a classic western oakwood, has a few great ashes in valley bottoms). Within a mixed area of woodland, ash trees are scattered apparently at random: the species is not clonal, forming circular patches like most elms, nor gregarious like lime and hornbeam, nor does it shun its own company like crab apple.

Ash trees grow almost everywhere except on soils that are both acid and infertile. Ashwoods occur on dry chalklands and wet fens; they hardly need soil, for they are found on limestone pavement and limestone scree. Ash does not prefer, as maple often does, to grow on the banks that delimit the edges of ancient woods.

Ancient woods in Europe have many different tree communities. The most comprehensive classification in Britain is by George Peterken in 1981, who published 59 'stand types' and variant tree communities. With others that I have added, this makes 68 tree communities of ancient woodland. Including rare types that we missed the total would probably be nearly 100. Out of the 68, 29 have ash as one of the defining species. Ash can be combined with almost all other trees (though rarely with birch); it contributes to the ways in which every ancient wood is uniquely different from every other.

Early ecologists were fascinated by the limestone ashwoods of the Mendips, Cotswolds, Derbyshire Dales and extending into Wales. C.E. Moss studied them more than a century ago in the first attempt at an ecological account of British woodland. Sir Arthur Tansley, in *The British Islands and their Vegetation* (1939), has a chapter on them as if they were the only ashwoods.

To describe ashwoods fully would fill a bigger book than this. The most widespread are those of the Ash–Maple–

Hazel group (ten of Peterken's variants), the normal coppice-woods of Midland England, most of East Anglia and north Essex. They are on moderately acid to weakly alkaline soils, often waterlogged during wet springs. Ash, maple and hazel form the underwood, mixed in almost any proportion. Nearly all woods of these types have (or have had) a scatter of oaks and sometimes ashes as timber trees. There is not much of a pattern about the relative proportions of ash, maple and hazel, except that maple tends to be on strongly clayey soils. However, in Hayley Wood, Cambridgeshire, ash tends to be more dominant in the flat part of the wood where rainwater collects in late winter, maple on slightly sloping parts where water runs away, and hazel in between. Ash does not grow better on the waterlogged site, but periodic waterlogging indirectly allows ash trees to get started. Waterlogging prevents dog's mercury from forming a continuous canopy, against which ashlings are worse competitors (*see* p.16) than maples.

In the chalklands of south England there is a different pattern. Valley bottoms tend to be cultivated land and meadow. The flat tops of the chalk ridges, with acid soils derived from loess and clay-with-flints, are wooded with oak or sometimes maple. The middle slopes, too steep for cultivation, have woods of ash or hazel. These are very distinctive: the breakneck slopes, sometimes hazardous with loose sharp flints; the patches of flint scree that chink underfoot; the huge old ash stools; near-absence of oak; the bluebells, toothwort on hazel stools, and occasional clonal patches of Herb Paris.

In north and west Britain a widespread type of woodland

on less acid soils are Peterken's Ash–Wych-Elm woods. In the late twentieth century the elms were hard hit by Elm Disease, but many of the stools recovered and are now an understorey to the enlarged ash trees.

In the Chilterns the great beechwoods are mainly on acid soils, but on chalk slopes beech is mixed with ash. Although beech is native here, it has been encouraged by people planting it in the belief that it is the 'natural' tree on chalk soils, and in the past the slopes may have had much more ash.

Ash is often thought of as the tree of non-acidic soils, but this is only a tendency. In my study of the woods of East Anglia and Essex in the 1970s and 1980s I found soil pH[2] under ash to range from 3.5 to 7.8, although it is less frequent on the more acidic soils. There is a rare type of woodland, Acid Ashwood, on sands and gravels north of Colchester: huge, widely spaced ash trees with scattered hazels, sparse bracken, and magnificent bluebells.

Ash is often associated with the lime tree. Although lime is a gregarious tree, so that woods tend to have patches of lime and patches of other trees, even dense lime areas may have standard trees of ash. Each time a lime area is coppiced there is a new crop of ash (rather than lime) seedlings. Most die in the dense shade, but some grow into young ash trees, and one or two survive the intense competition of the lime regrowth and become big trees.

Further north and west, in areas with higher rainfall and

2 pH is a measure of soil acidity. In Britain it ranges from 3.0 in the most acid soils to 8.2 in the most alkaline. Here it was measured with a glass electrode against solutions of standard pH. Soils could now be less acidic, now that acid rain has diminished.

Fig. 20 Primrose is a coppicing plant, flourishing in the years after the wood is felled. It is abundant under ash and other trees including lime. Buff Wood, Cambridgeshire, April 1969.

more leached soils, ash tends to be confined either to the bottoms of slopes – into which minerals have been washed from the oakwoods above – or to limestone outcrops and cliffs. In Rassall Ashwood near Loch Kishorn, huge veteran ash trees (apparently not coppice or pollards), some well over 200 years old, grow on limestone knobs and stone-piles. This is a National Nature Reserve and a scheduled archaeological site; the relation between the trees and the copper mining and Iron Age features is still unknown.

Ashwoods have a huge range of woodland plants under them. Almost any are possible, although plants of acid soils – bracken, foxglove, wood sage – are rare under ash, as are

Fig. 21 Buried-seed plants include ragged robin (pink) and lesser spearwort (yellow). Very many such plants emerge from a seed-bank every time the wood is felled. Even more than perennial coppicing plants, they vary erratically from one wood to the next and are not linked to any specific tree. Hayley Wood, Cambridgeshire, June 1988.

plants of more fertile soils – nettle, ground ivy, cow parsley. It is less obvious why wood anemone tends to avoid ash.

Woods of ash, like other trees, have many plants that do not prosper under continuous shade but flourish every time the wood is cut down. Some, like primrose and bluebell, are long-lived, waxing and waning with the coppicing and regrowth of the wood (Fig. 20). Others, like ragged robin and wood spurge, are not visible all the time: at each felling they reappear (Fig. 21) from buried seed, shed after the previous felling. Yet others, like marsh thistle, move round the wood from one felled area to another. Ash is probably less prolific in these 'coppicing plants' than trees like hornbeam and lime that cast a denser shade for a longer part of the year.

Ash in recent woodland

Very many woodland plants are characteristic of ancient woodland – woods that have existed for several centuries – and, for various reasons, do not easily get into new woodland. Among trees these include lime and service. Ash is not like this.

Whenever a field or quarry or industrial site is abandoned it is soon taken over by trees and turns into a wood. Ash is one of the common trees that do this. If I were to abandon my garden in Cambridge it would be an ash-holly wood within ten years. In the coalfield valleys of South Wales, which between the wars had little woodland, ash is now abundant on former mining sites and derelict railways. However, it will be decades or centuries before a new ashwood that extends an existing wood acquires all the herbaceous plants of established woodland, and longer still if the new wood is isolated in the middle of fields.

The densest stand of ash that I have seen is next to Arger-Fen Wood in Suffolk. This is a field that was acquired by Suffolk Wildlife Trust in 1994, ploughed, then left. Up to 300 yards from the original wood is a wood exclusively of young ashes so crowded that I had to squeeze sideways between them (Fig. 22). The old wood is mainly of cherry, but there is not a single specimen in the new wood. Further out the ash gives way to birch, uncommon in the old wood.

Fig. 22 Extremely dense ashwood, arisen spontaneously on what was a field 19 years ago. Note dark 'sock' of mosses at base of each tree.

Like other trees, ash competes with grass for nitrogen compounds and water. When myxomatosis was let loose in Britain in 1954, killing nearly all the rabbits, the sudden reduction in grazing is said to have been unfavourable to ash because the grass was stimulated. Rabbits have long since recovered, but grass competition can hold back new woodland from forming on abandoned fields.

Ash plantations

Ash, although it grows very well spontaneously from seed, is commonly planted – so commonly as to expose it to imported tree diseases (*see* Chapter 6). Ash is sometimes planted by itself, but since the 1970s it appears as a component of a 'standard broadleaf mixture' with oak, cherry, lime, etc. – a generic, heavy-handed attempt to replicate the composition of native woodland.

Fig. 23 A late twentieth-century 'broadleaf mix' plantation on what 20 years before was a field. Dorset, March 2014.

Ash plantations tend to be dull and repetitive (Fig. 23), lacking the diverse shapes and sizes of trees and coppice stools that make ash part of the rich variety of 'real' woodland. Like other plantations, they have herbaceous plants of well-fertilised land – cow parsley, nettle etc. – although a few have spectacular stands of bluebells. Plantations of other trees, if neglected, tend to lose the planted trees and turn into stands of self-sown ash or birch.

Ash in wood-pasture

Historically, wood-pasture has been one of the main types of tree-land in England and especially Scotland, often in a form in which trees – often pollarded – were scattered in grassland or heath, as in Ashtead Common or Burnham Beeches, or in the savannas of Africa, Australia and the Wild West of North America. For the last 900 years this has taken three forms: *wooded commons*, in which local farmers had communal rights of pasture and sometimes woodcutting; *parks*, private wood-pastures for keeping semi-domestic deer; and *wooded Forests*, areas on which the king (or some other great magnate) had the right to keep deer in addition to the livestock of commoners. (The word Forest, with a capital F, implies deer rather than trees: some Forests were wooded, like Epping Forest, and some not, like Dartmoor Forest.)

It might be thought that ash, being palatable, would be at a disadvantage in wood-pasture, especially in Forests which were usually on the acid soils that ash often avoids. There is some evidence for this: thus there are two surveys of underwood in coppices (that is, woods that were periodically felled and then fenced to keep out the livestock until the trees had grown again) in Rockingham Forest, Northamptonshire, in 1564–5. Out of 187 coppices, ash is recorded in only 26, whereas thorn appears in 182 and maple in 143. Being in a Forest is a factor that encourages maple at the expense of ash. In the same way, detailed censuses of trees on the Hatfield estate, Hertfordshire, in the sixteenth century record only one ash among thousands of oak, beech and hornbeam pollards in the wood-pastures, but many ashes among pollard trees in farmland.

Wood-pastures on non-acid soils can have ash, as in Wychwood Forest, Oxfordshire, where there may have been a long period without deer, allowing ash to recover. In Hatfield Forest, Essex, there are a few ancient picturesque pollard ashes. Ashes are among the very few relics of the once countless pollards of Ettrick Forest in south-east Scotland. In the Highlands of Scotland, on less acidic rocks, ash often

Fig. 24 A little-known aspect of ash: trees that are scattered savanna-like in grassland and moorland in the Highlands of Scotland. Glen Lyon, Perthshire, 2010.

grows as scattered trees in grassland (Fig. 24). The trees tend to be middle-aged, and correspond to rock outcrops or small pits that break the surface of the grass.

Ash in hedges and fields

Ash is not only a hedgerow tree, but one of the common constituents of the hedge itself. It is not a particularly desirable constituent, being of little use in maintaining a stock-proof barrier, and so it is rare to find a hedge all of ash. Ash easily gets into a hawthorn hedge. Outside Hayley

Wood, a hawthorn hedge was planted in 1970 parallel to an existing mixed hedge containing ash, a lane's-width apart. The first ashes appeared in the new hedge after only 11 years. The situation was exceptionally favourable to ash invasion; elsewhere it might have been a century or more before ash appeared.

As in woodland, individual hedgerow ashes persist indefinitely and form huge stools. If the hedge has been managed by coppicing, like a linear wood, ash stools may grow to 6 feet or more across along the length of the hedge. Where there is a tradition of *plashing* or *laying* the hedge – cutting part-way through the stems and bending them over to form a horizontal barrier – this permanently alters the architecture of ash and other trees. The plashed stems may grow over the centuries into massive horizontal trunks extending 10 feet or more on either side of the original stool (Fig. 25).

Ash on rock and buildings

Ash, like many trees, will grow on the thinnest of soils or without soil. A preferred habitat is on cliffs, dry-stone walls, screes, stone-piles and ruins, especially on limestone (Fig. 26). A famous example is Colt Park Wood in north-west Yorkshire, where ash trees are rooted in the fissures of limestone pavement. Ash on a cliff can form a massive woody base, a *lignotuber*. Rocks may reduce competition between grasses and the infant tree, and may give it some protection against grazing.

Ash is not much of an inner-city tree, for it does not appeal to formal planters. It is common in outer cities, in big gardens and odd pieces of abandoned land. In my childhood

Fig. 25 Enormous ash stool in the remains of a woodland-edge hedge in Powerstock Common, Dorset, April 2011. The horizontal boughs result from a history of plashing.

Fig. 26 Ash is one of those trees that do not need soil to grow on, evident in these stunted specimens rooted in the limestone pavement. Burren, County Clare, Ireland.

Fig. 27 The Hardy Ash Tree, St Pancras Churchyard, London. Thomas Hardy studied architecture in London from 1862 to 1867, during which time he oversaw the careful removal of bodies and tombs from land on which the Midland Railway line was being built.

I tried to teach myself ecology in the ruins of Norwich, eight to ten years after the Blitz. Although trees were already growing on stumps of lime-mortared walls and heaps of rubble, ash was rare: the common trees were elder, sycamore and (surprisingly) aspen.

2 The ash tree in prehistory and history

> ... to the stock on which a hinged gate hangs; from the stock out through Birchley midwards to the old ash; from the ash south over the way to the apple tree; from the apple tree to the white hazel; from the hazel to Nutwick eastward; along the green way to the horn of Wuhingland ...

> *Perambulation of Havant (Hants)*, dated 980
> [horn: narrow corner projection where a road enters a common]

Origins of ash

THE WORLDWIDE plant family Oleaceæ, which includes ash, olive, privet, lilac, etc., presumably originated in dinosaur time, at least 200 million years ago. Then nearly all the world's land was joined up in the supercontinent Pangæa. The break-up of this land mass carried members of the Oleaceæ to all the habitable continents.

The genus *Fraxinus*, the ash trees, may have begun in east Asia, at least 130 million years ago, and spread into Europe and North America when there was a land connection across the Bering Strait. There is now one species in north and middle Europe, three others in southern Europe, twenty-one species in North America (which may, partly, result from American botanists' different attitude to what constitutes a species), five in Japan, and others in mainland Asia.

The ancestors of ash evolved in response to slow changes in the environment and in the animals that preyed on them. By two million years ago, this process produced something like the present species of ash. Then evolution was rudely interrupted by climate change: by the comparatively rapid cycles known as the ice ages. *Interglacial* periods of several thousand years, with a climate rather like the present, alternated with longer *glacial* periods when trees could not live in Britain. During interglacials trees returned to these islands from refugia in southern Europe. They formed part of the *wildwood*, natural vegetation as yet not altered by organised human activity.

Wildwood

The composition of wildwood is known from pollen preserved in permanently wet places like lake mud and peat bogs. Ash, although partly wind-pollinated, appears to have been under-represented compared to oak and hazel. Even allowing for meagre pollen production, it then appears to have been uncommon in the wildwood of previous interglacials, although pollen sites are few and may have missed places where ash was abundant.

The present interglacial period, the *Holocene*, began about 12,000 years ago. In human terms this was the late Palæolithic: people like you and me, modern *Homo sapiens*, were making a living by hunting, trapping and gathering and using wooden tools. The first trees to appear after the last Ice Age were pine and birch, then hazel. Ash appears relatively early but sparsely, slowly increasing in distribution and abundance.

By the fifth millennium BC, in the late Mesolithic, wildwood was dominated by lime in lowland England, by oak and hazel in Wales, western England, and south Scotland, by elm and hazel in most of Ireland, and birch and pine in the Scottish

Highlands. Ash was widespread but usually only a minor constituent. However, in some sites in Norfolk and northern England, ash was the co-dominant or dominant tree. The reconstruction that emerges is of ash trees scattered among limewoods, oakwoods, elmwoods and hazelwoods, plus occasional patches of ashwood in favoured spots.

What did wildwood look like? The traditional reconstruction of trees, trees, trees and trees cannot be sustained. There must have been *some* permanent open areas, because there was pollen of plants like devil's-bit scabious that do not flower in shade. Frans Vera has an alternative reconstruction of wildwood as a patchwork of areas of woodland and areas of grassland in which the grazing of deer and wild oxen played a critical part, forever shifting as grassland was invaded by trees and trees died in woodland and were replaced by grassland. This is not the place to argue which reconstruction is right. Ash, as a tree of new woodland (*see* p.41), could have invaded grassland, although palatability (*see* p.24) would have worked against it.

The Holocene had more ash and more hazel than previous interglacials. Why was this so? There were two peculiarities that may be linked: the presence of *Homo sapiens*, and the absence of giant beasts. Previously there had been superelephants: not the puny monsters of Whipsnade, but creatures of Tolkienesque size and majesty like the West Runton elephant, that could break down and devour a big tree. Did these living bulldozers hold down ash in previous interglacials? Or could Mesolithic people in some way have favoured ash?

Why (in evolutionary terms) do trees like ash sprout when

felled? What did they do with this property before people invented axes? Not all trees have it. Coppicing is not a fire adaptation: pines, for which fire is part of their normal life cycle, do not coppice, whereas ash, a most difficult tree to set on fire, does. Was it part of the damage-repair mechanisms by which trees responded (and still respond at Whipsnade) to elephant attack?

Ash of prehistory

Around 4000 BC there began a new human lifestyle: growing crops, keeping domestic animals, building houses, temples and tombs, making pottery, and the other trappings of settled civilisation. This is marked in the pollen record by a sudden decline of elm all over north-west Europe. The Elm Decline has been ascribed to people pollarding elms for leaves to feed livestock because, in (supposedly) continuous forest, there was no grassland (Fig. 28). Pollarded elms would have produced much less pollen. If so, there ought to be an Ash Decline at the same time, because ash leaves are just as good, but there is not. Although the tree that benefited from the subtraction of elm is usually hazel, in some places it is ash that takes elm's place. The Elm Decline is now known to have taken (at most) four years, which makes disease the only plausible cause.

Neolithic people began slowly to convert wildwood (or, on Vera's theory, at first the open areas within wildwood) to the fields, pastures, heaths and moorland of historic times. England passed the stage of being half forest probably at some time in the Bronze or early Iron Age – roughly between 1300 and 700 BC. Ash benefited: its pollen increases at many

Fig. 28 *Shredding* is a variant of pollarding to get leaves to feed livestock. Elm is generally preferred, but ash comes next, as pictured here. Before the Iron Age invention of the scythe made it feasible to harvest and store hay, leaf-fodder would have been necessary wherever grass did not grow all the year round. It is still made in scattered parts of Europe. Sognefjord, Norway, July 1986.

sites. Farmland would have retreated as well as advancing, giving ash opportunities to occupy abandoned land.

Meanwhile the remaining wildwood was used, and some was converted to managed woodland. Giant forest trees were of little use to people without power tools, except for

Fig. 29 Twelve years of excavation revealed the woodland crafts that created this Neolithic trackway across the Somerset Levels. This and later trackways were made of hazel, oak, alder and ash.

making dugout boats, for which ash was rarely used. More useful were the coppice poles that grew from the stumps of felled trees.

Evidence for the use of ash begins with Neolithic trackways excavated in the Somerset Levels, for example the Sweet Track, dated to *c.*3800 BC (Fig. 29). These are of varied construction, some being made of wattle hurdles, others of planks and posts. Ash appears in many, but was not preferred; it forms at most one-tenth of the components.

Fig. 30 Bronze Age wood-working tools: did the socketed gouge and tanged chisels have ash handles? From J. Forde-Johnston, *Prehistoric Britain and Ireland* (1976).

Some of the ash poles are definitely from coppice; they have an incomplete last annual ring, showing that they were felled in summer, probably as a by-product of harvesting leaves for fodder.

The Bronze Age waterfront structures excavated at Caldicot, Monmouthshire, also used a small proportion of ash. Here the trees had often been timber-sized, being divided and worked with bronze tools. The carpenters had mastered the rather difficult art of splitting ash to produce planks. The giant causeway and artificial island at Flag Fen, Peterborough, the biggest timber structure ever built in these islands, uses very little, if any, ash.

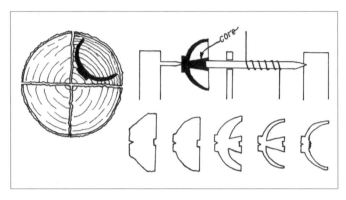

Fig. 31 The craft of cupping. How the cup sits in the original tree; diagram of a cupper's lathe; stages in making the cup.

Among the uses for which ash was later preferred, tool handles can be traced back to a Bronze Age axe-haft at Flag Fen. Iron Age wheels of *c.*500 BC have been found in the chariot burials of East Yorkshire. The ring of the wheel is said to be of ash bent into a circle with only one join, and reinforced with a continuous iron tyre. The secret of the continuous tyre was lost and not recovered until the eighteenth century, and the secret of the one-piece ring has never been recovered.

An odd artefact made from ash, but for no obvious reason, was the carved case containing a pair of shears in the Bronze Age of Flag Fen.

Ash in early historic times

Ash was much used in Viking Dublin (Wood Quay), even for the massive timbers of door frames set in the ground where they would not last long. At York, the Coppergate

('Cuppers' Street') excavation revealed the factories of cup-turners, *c.*950–1150 AD, in which ash was the commonest material (*see* p.94); similar ashen bowls have been found in Cork, Ireland. A short log, a little longer than the diameter of the cup and about twice as thick, would be cleft into four, and each quarter mounted in a lathe and made into a cup or bowl (Fig. 31). It would be no good making a vessel out of a whole log because it would crack along the radius.

Ash and thorn are the commonest trees in English place-names from the first millennium AD (*see* Chapter 4), as in Ashton and Thornham. The earliest precise records of ash trees are in Anglo-Saxon charters dating from 600 to 1080 AD. Before maps, land conveyances defined the estate by a *perambulation* of the boundaries in terms of rivers, roads, hedges, trees, antiquities, etc. By my reckoning, they mention 658 trees, mostly in the tenth century. Thorn is strongly predominant (40%), followed by oak (13%) and apple or crab (10%). Ash accounts for only 7%, along with willow and elder. Ash is most often mentioned in Somerset charters. The earliest mention of an identifiable ash tree in Britain appears to be 'one ash' at Tangmere, Sussex, in 680.

Charter bounds are mostly through farmland, not woodland. They record the ordinary trees of hedges and watercourses, including ash, along with maple and alder. Ash is not associated either with well-wooded or poorly-wooded parts of England. Usually it is just 'ash', along with features named after ash, such as springs and streams called Ashwell, or barrows and forts called Ashbury. Sometimes it is 'great ash', 'high ash', 'old ash', 'ash stump', or 'ashstead', presumably the place where an ash tree used to be. There is a 'hollow ash', a 'holed ash' and an 'ivied ash'. In four instances an ash or an ash stump was recognisable enough to be the point where a perambulation began and finished.

Ash in the Middle Ages and after

Before the sixteenth century written records of ash (as of other tree species except oak and elm) are sparse, although most well-documented places have some. Mostly, they appear to be outside woodland. Ash occurred in woods, but is lost in the anonymity of underwood, whose composition is seldom recorded. In a wood in Writtle Forest, Essex, in 1406–7, 37 ashes were felled to make hoops (*see* p.98). In Hatfield Forest, Essex, and the adjacent park in 1443, 67 ash trees were sold to 18 people for an average of 17 pence (£70 in the money of 2014) each, so they must have been substantial timber trees; whether they were in woodland is not stated.

Records sometimes refer to special trees: a thirteenth-century land grant at Great Wenham, Suffolk, excepted 'the great ash standing on the said land'. A map of Dodnash Wood, not far away, in 1634, singles out 'Two great ashes'; and there are still two great ash trees (not the same ones!) in this generally unfavourable wood.[1]

There have been Epistle Oaks and Gospel Oaks, usually on parish boundaries where the epistle and gospel of the day would be read during the annual beating of the bounds. Liturgical ashes are fewer, but a place called Gospel Ash became the site of Wolverhampton Airport, and an actual Gospel Ash is said to survive on the Somerset–Dorset

---

1 Suffolk Record Office (Ipswich): ESRO: B1/11 Shelf 19.

boundary near Purse Caundle.

England has had vast numbers of hedgerow and field trees, especially in the period 1500–1750. Surveys of non-woodland trees from the thirteenth to the nineteenth centuries list oak, ash and elm, less often willow. At Hindolveston, Norfolk, in 1255–1327, ash was the commonest hedgerow tree, followed by willow, with oak confined to woods and no mention of elm. In 1442, someone was fined for cutting down a mixed hedge in Hatfield Broadoak, Essex, containing ash trees. At Tanworth, Warwickshire, in c.1500, a survey records over 2,000 timber trees, nearly all in hedges, including 1,215 oaks and 594 ashes. At Thorndon, Suffolk, in 1742, on 187 acres of farmland, there were 7,360 trees (more to the acre than timber trees in most woods), two-thirds being oak and one-sixth each ash and elm. Ash, like oak or elm, could be either timber or pollard or coppice. Where non-woodland trees were thick on the ground, as at Thorndon, they were mostly pollarded.

Ash is among the earliest non-fruit trees known to be planted. In the fourteenth century, as now, there was no need to buy ash plants. Ashes up to at least three years old can be pulled up in fields and gardens and moved to where they are wanted. In 1312–3, the monks of Norwich Cathedral were planting large quantities of ashes on their manor of Hindringham: they employed two men for a week to pull them on another estate at Hindolveston, and one man for a week to plant them.[2] At Forncett, Norfolk, in 1378, a new hedge was planted using pulled plants of thorn and ash.

2 Norfolk and Norwich Record Office: Dean and Chapter Rolls 4755, 4899.

There was a nursery trade in plants of garden trees, but with ash it seems to have been unnecessary.

Later, ash is more often recorded within as well as outside woodland. In the Middle Ages, the meagre evidence suggests that ash timber trees were more valuable than oak of the same size, but by the eighteenth century they sold for about two-thirds the price of oak per cubic foot. Like oak, the price of ash timber tended to increase by rather more than the rate of inflation.

Ash coppice stools are an independent witness in woodland and hedges. Coppice stools of a size indicating that they are medieval (Fig. 32 and *see* Fig. 25, page 47) are found in most types of ashwood, but usually only a minority are so big; they are outnumbered by smaller stools a century or two old. In some woods, such as parts of the Bradfield Woods, Suffolk, there are many ancient ash stools, showing that ash has been dominant for centuries.

Another independent witness is timber and underwood in ancient buildings. Timbers in English historic carpentry are oak, elm, aspen, ash, black poplar and imported pine. Oak (partly imported) is commoner than elm; elm is commoner than ash. Partly this is due to the rot-resistance of oak: ash timbers, and buildings made of them, are less likely to survive, although aspen, even less durable, is no less common than ash. Ash rots quickly when exposed to the weather. Kept dry, like most timbers, it lasts indefinitely: the oldest ash timbers in houses are still going strong after more than 700 years.

Ash is never found in church carpentry and other high-status uses (though I am told of an all-ash church roof in Poland). There are written records of ash carpentry, for

Fig. 32 A great ash stool on an ancient earthwork. Chrishall Park Wood, Essex, April 2013.

example in the Furness Abbey accounts of 1438, but actual finds are mainly in Suffolk and Norfolk. Ash, the third-best timber, often appears in low-status uses where the kind of timber did not matter much. Thus in Valley Farm, Flatford, Suffolk, a middle-class house of *c.*1400 (Fig. 33), most of the timber frame is oak and elm, but in the service rooms there is some ash, mainly in places away from the weather – along with recycled oak. The ash timbers are sawn from middle-sized trees and retain their bark (with breeding galleries of

Fig. 33 Valley Farm, Flatford. House of *c.*1400. The timber frame is made partly of recycled oak, odds and ends of new oak, elm, ash and poplar, indications of economy. The interstices of the timber frame are filled with underwood in the form of wattle-and-daub.

Fig. 34 Ash timber in Valley Farm. Some of the bark has fallen away revealing breeding galleries of one of the ash bark beetles, made within months of the tree being felled.

ash bark beetle, Fig. 34). Close by, at Songers in Boxted, one of the oldest small houses in England, dated to *c.*1280, is built round four posts sawn lengthwise out of the same ash tree. Excavation of medieval houses at the waterlogged site of Coppergate, York, revealed a few ash among the carpentry timbers. Ash timber is more common in later buildings down to the eighteenth century, usually as scattered components rather than a whole building.

Ash underwood appears in historic buildings more often than timber, as wattle – the coppice rods, variously interwoven, that fill the panels between the timbers. In East Anglia, where the tree species evidently did not matter much, I find that 18 per cent of the wattle rods are ash; less than sallow and hazel, more than aspen. Ash may form a whole wattle panel or be mixed with other species.

3 Veteran, ancient and exceptional ash trees

> how oft a summer shower has started me
> to seek the shelter of a hollow tree
> old huge ash dotterel wasted to a shell
> whose vigorous head still grew and flourished well
> where ten might sit upon the battered floor
> and still look round discovering room for more
>
> JOHN CLARE, *c.*1825

TREES GROWN FOR TIMBER are typically felled at one-quarter or less of their natural longevity. Beyond this age they develop cavities, dead branches, bulges, burrs, overhangs and other features. These 'defects' spoil their commercial value, but make a tree's individuality and its value as a habitat. Youngish trees are all much the same. Veteran ashes harbour hole-nesting birds, bats (different species roost and breed in different parts of the tree), special lichens (those that live on old dry bark or on rainwater tracks), special mosses and liverworts, and all the insects that inhabit rotten wood, loose bark and wet rot-holes, and the spiders that prey on the insects. One 200-year-old ash can be a series of ecosystems for which 10,000 50-year-old ashes are no use at all.

Veteran trees – roughly, those in the last three-quarters of their lives – harbour most of the cultural and spiritual values of trees: sacred trees, named trees, trees on maps, memorable trees, pollards and the host of trees modified by past practices.

Fig. 35 An 'old huge ash dotterel': ancient pollard ash in Glanvilles Wootton, Dorset. Note the mouldering interior, and the lichens covering and hiding the rugged bark.

A subset of veteran trees is *ancient trees*, older individuals with more accumulation of ecological and cultural values. Neither are necessarily *champion* or especially big trees.

What are veteran trees?

Because veteran trees have no timber interest their functioning has been neglected. It was once thought that decay was a disease to be prevented: anyone cutting a branch had to paint

Fig. 36 'The Great Ash at Carnock' from Jacob Strutt's *Sylva Britannica*.

the scar with a tarry compound, failing which wood-rotting fungi would enter and eat away the tree until it fell down.

Trees have no immune system like vertebrate animals, but they have a damage-limitation mechanism. When a tree is injured, or sheds a redundant twig, or is attacked by a fungus such as *Chalara* (*see* Chapter 5), its wood responds by developing *compartment barriers*, depending on the location and size of the wound or infection. Wood-rotting fungi enter the cut or broken surface (whether anointed or not) and consume the wood up to the barrier (Fig. 35). With a big hollow tree this may take years, providing successive habitats for veteran-tree animals. The tree gets rid of wood no longer needed to hold it up, recycling the minerals in that wood back to the roots. (Hornbeam and willow sprout new roots into the disintegrating core of redundant wood.) Normally, decay does not spread into wood formed after the original injury. A mouldering interior is part of normal development in most trees, comparable to grey hair or increasing wisdom in the human species.

Finally, a hollow tree is created, strong enough to withstand the Great Storm of 1987 that uprooted or broke many youngish trees. It has a hard inner lining that may remain stable for centuries until superseded by a new barrier when some fresh damage occurs. A pollard tree forms a new barrier each time the tree is cut.[1]

Ancient coppice stools

By convention, recorders of veteran trees count standard trees and pollards, excluding the hollow coppiced stools in ancient woodland and hedges. This is illogical: stools are the most numerous old ash trees and probably include the very oldest (Fig. 37). They perform some functions of veteran trees, especially the above-ground bases, which are a bryophyte habitat.

How old are they? In the destructive 1970s ash stools could be dated by finding where foresters, intending to destroy the

1 The wood-rotting fungus *Inonotus hispidus* can break through these compartment barriers, and is often associated with breakage of ash (*see* Fig. 15, page 29).

stool, had cut through the hollow base, sectioning annual rings from the last few coppice cycles (Fig. 38). At each coppicing (or pollarding) there is a sudden setback to the tree's growth, followed by a gradual recovery as the canopy is restored.

Table 1 Coppice cycles as recorded by the annual rings of an ash stool, Hayley Wood, Cambridgeshire.

1785 (earliest visible)	1798 (31 years)	1813 (15 years)
1826 (13 years)	1841 (15 years)	1869 (28 years)
1886 (17 years)	1905 (19 years)	1915 (10 years)

Dating is not an exact science, especially as a small stool can be a fragment of what was once much bigger. Roughly, a stool 5 feet in diameter is likely to be at least 400 years old, and one 9 feet in diameter at least 800 years. (The stool of Table 1 was only 16 inches in diameter and was about 270 years old when investigated.)

What constitutes one stool? The young stems and leaves of ash are tinged orange or purple. The pigment may colour the whole shoot and leaves, or be confined to rings round lenticels, or be distributed in other ways. All the shoots on one stool share the same pattern. Big coppice stools often split into separate sectors, and this is useful in determining whether two parts are the same or different individuals (Fig. 39). Usually it confirms that a big stool is one tree, but occasionally parts of a stool have different pigmentations, proving that it is two individuals coalesced. This is best observed in the first year of regrowth, but even after many

Fig. 37 The biggest known ash stool? This individual is probably much older than any upstanding ash tree. The lack of an above-ground base is unusual. Paynsden Wood, Quendon, Essex, 1971.

Fig. 38 In the bad old days sections of ash stools were often available as a means of studying their annual rings. Westonbirt Arboretum (site of Silk Wood), Gloucestershire, March 1980.

Fig. 39 A big old ash stool in its first year of regrowth after felling. The pigmentation marks out this ash as one individual. Every shoot has a deep purple stem and a reddish tinge to the young leaves.

years some peculiarity of shape or branching habit or bark detail may establish whether or not an outlying sector belongs to a nearby stool.

Notable ash trees

Ancient ash trees have been remarked in English landscapes at least since an 'old ash' boundary tree in Taunton, Somerset, and a 'hollow ash' in Farleigh Chamberlayne, Hampshire, both in 980.

John Clare, labourer-poet (1793–1864), wrote in sorrow and anger at the catastrophic effects of the Enclosure Act of 1809 on the landscape of Helpston, Northamptonshire. The heaths and lanes of his childhood had been replaced by ordinary fields like anywhere else, and the wonderful pollards lingering from the Middle Ages had been wantonly destroyed:

> when in round oaks narrow lane as the south got black again
> we sought the hollow ash that was shelter from the rain
> with our pockets full of pease we had stolen from the grain
>
> .   .   .   .   .   .
>
> o words are poor reciepts for what time hath stole away
> the ancient pulpit trees and the play.

In the half of England that escaped Enclosure Acts such trees, or their successors, are still to be found. Even in places like Helpston a new generation of veteran ashes, though less impressive than Clare's, has now arisen.

Jacob Strutt's *Sylva Britannica* of 1822 is a book of portraits of ancient or famous trees, most of which are oaks. Strutt was too late to record Clare's pulpit trees and has only two ashes, at Woburn Park in Bedfordshire and Carnock in

Fig. 40 Exceptional ancient ash tree at Moccas Park, Herefordshire.

Fig. 41 Other countries and continents have veteran ash trees. Here is one in the Wild West, probably *Fraxinus pensylvanica*. Valley Mills, Texas, December 2012.

Fig. 42 Ancient coppice stool of ash, converted into a ring of pollards. Ire, Blekinge, Sweden, September 2000.

Fig. 43 Old pollard ashes, like this one languishing in the depths of a forestry plantation, often originated on boundary walls in farmland and are typical of those in highland regions of England and Wales. Dyffryn Crawnon, Breconshire, 2007.

Stirlingshire (Fig. 36). These were simply huge trees and not otherwise special. The Carnock Ash was claimed to have been planted by a Lord Advocate of Scotland in *c.*1596.

Loudon's encyclopædic *Arboretum* lists notable trees. He mentions a few ashes, mostly in Scotland – fewer than notable oaks, of which he has dozens of little portraits, or elms, beeches, chestnuts and willows. He records unusually fast-grown ashes, and seems not to have appreciated ash pollards. A little later, Grigor's book on remarkable trees in Norfolk (1841) has 48 portraits of interesting trees, five being ashes, including two weeping ash (*see* Fig. 19, pages 34–35).

Exceptional ash trees (*see* Table 2) are mostly in parks, never in woods, and are especially in Scotland and Ireland.

Table 2 Some notable ash trees, excluding coppice stools
Those in *italics* are no longer extant

* Where known

Date	County	Site	Girth & point*	Height*	
c.1760[f]	Inverness, Scotland	*Kilmallie on Loch Eil*	58 ft at ground		Sacred tree, destroyed 1746
1808[e]	Galway, Ireland	*Doriney near Claregalway*	42 ft at 4 ft		School in its hollow interior
2010[d]	Carmarthen, Wales	Talley Abbey	33½ ft		
2013[a]	Tipperary, Ireland	Ardfert House	33 ft at 5 ft	95 ft	
1838[f]	Dunbarton, Scotland	*Bonhill*	34 ft at 4 ft		Room built in interior
1883[b]	Perth, Scotland	*Logierait*	32 ft 5 in at 5 ft		
2013[a]	Perth, Scotland	Ochtertyre, Crieff	29 ft at 3 ft		
1994[a]	Somerset, England	Clapton Court	27 ft at 5 ft	39 ft	Big-belly shape
1997[h]	Hereford, England	Moccas Park	26 ft 6 in	c.45 ft	Giraffe pollard
c.2000	Moray, Scotland	Gordon Castle	25 ft		
1792[b]	Laois, Ireland	*[Abbey]leix*	25 ft at 6 ft		
2010[d]	Hampshire	Torberry Hill	23 ft		'Trysting Tree'
1794[b]	Waterford, Ireland	*Curraghmore*	22 ft 6 in at 13 ft 9 in		
1906[b]	Carmarthen, Wales	*Dynenor Park*	22 ft 9 in	104 ft	

Date	Location	Place	Girth	Height	Notes
1838[f]	Hereford, England	*Moccas Park?*	21 ft at 15 ft		1003 cubic feet of timber
1841[c]	Norfolk, England	*Kimberley*	21 ft 2 in at 5 ft	82 ft	
c.1808[e]	Offaly, Ireland	*Kinnity*	21 ft		Sacred tree
1834	Tipperary, Ireland	*Tombrickane*	22 ft at base		The Twisted Ash
1838[f]	Kent, England	*Cobham Park*	20 ft 11 in	120 ft	
1822[g]	Stirling, Scotland	*Carnock*	19 ft 3 in at 5 ft	90 ft	Said to be planted c.1596, died c.1860
1822[g]	Bedford, England	*Woburn Park*	15 ft 3 in 3 ft	90 ft	873 cubic feet of timber
1848[e]	Cornwall, England	*Cury, Lizard*	14 ft at 5 ft		'Cury Great Tree' formerly haunt of wreckers
1906[b]	Kent, England	*Cobham Park*	13 ft	146 ft	Said to be 2nd tallest tree in England
1906	Selkirk, Scotland	*Yarrow*			Pollard
c.2000	Selkirk, Scotland	*Tinnis*			Pollard

Sources (*see* Bibliography for full references)

a Champion Trees (www.treeregister.org)

b Elwes and Henry published 1906

c Grigor published 1841

d Della Hooke

e C.A. Johns published 1869

f Loudon published 1841

g Strutt published 1838

f Tom Wall

Fig. 44 Hayley Wood, Cambridgeshire, May 1976: work begins on making new veteran trees (*above*) by cutting ex-coppice ash as pollards. After one year's growth (*below left*) fallow deer have eaten all the sprouts below a browse-line; cloven hoofmarks showed where they had tried to climb higher. In November 2007 (*below right*), 31 years and three pollard cycles later, the pollard ashes are beginning to develop the characteristics of veteran trees.

An extant example is the great ash of Moccas Park, Herefordshire. In this park, among the mysterious pollard 'old oak men', there is one ancient ash: a mighty tower of a tree, 'giraffe-pollarded' at some 25 feet above ground, with a massive swollen base and capacious hollow interior (Fig. 40). Others, taking the more usual form of a huge spreading tree, are the ashes of Whyddon Park on the edge of Dartmoor. Huge spreading trees may not be as old as one might expect from their girth.

A new generation of veteran ashes

Although *ancient* ash trees (other than coppice stools) are not in ancient woodland, woods are beginning to acquire veteran ashes. In Hayley Wood, where few timber trees have been felled since the 1920s, standard ashes are going hollow and developing veteran characteristics. Although of no great size, they are older than they look, some being well over 200. Their narrow annual rings show that an adverse environment, in this case wet soil, promotes longevity.

In Hayley Wood, early attempts to revive coppicing were frustrated by fallow deer, which had settled in the wood since historic coppicing had been abandoned. From 1975 onwards, ex-coppiced ashes were made into pollards, cut at 6–7 feet above ground instead of near ground level (Fig. 44). They sprouted all up the remaining trunk, but the deer ate the sprouts as high as they could reach. After three successive pollardings in less than 40 years they have compartmentalised into hollow interiors with mouldering dead wood tunnelled by the Lesser Stag-Beetle. They are well on the way to becoming veteran trees.

4 Cultural, spiritual and material ash

As to [ash's] toughness and elasticity . . . it is only necessary
to look to the articles made from it by the sievewright and
the basket-maker, in whose hands ash-wood bends like a
piece of wire.

J. BROWN, *The Forester*, 1882

A SH HAS UNRELATED NAMES in the different families of
European languages: Germanic-Scandinavian (*Esche,
aske*), Celtic (*onnen, uinnius*), Romance (*fraxinus, frêne*), Greek
(*melía*). The Turks, coming probably from a part of Central
Asia that had no ash trees nor a word for them, invented a
nickname, *dişbudak*, 'tooth-twig' (was ash one of the trees
whose twigs have been used as toothbrushes?).

'Ash' has been applied also to unrelated but vaguely similar
trees, like mountain-ash or rowan and American prickly-ash,
Xanthoxylum americanum, both of which have ash-like leaves.
The Australian mountain-ashes, eucalypts which are among
the world's tallest trees, are unrelated and do not resemble ash.

Place-names

The earliest written records are in English place-names.
Names of towns, villages and hamlets often refer to trees,
like Maplestead, Sevenoaks, etc. Most of them were already
there by Domesday Book (1086), and sporadic earlier records
show that many go back to the early Anglo-Saxon period,
seventh century or before.

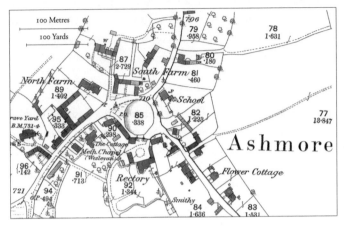

Fig. 45 Ashmore, Dorset–Wiltshire border, named after the hilltop pond, the Ash-Mere (85 on the map), now in the middle of the village.

Among trees in place-names, ash and thorn (hawthorn and blackthorn) – Ashmore, Aston, Thornham and their like – are the commonest: each accounts for 18 per cent of 812 place-names. They are followed by willow and then oak.

What does this mean? These must be trees of settlements, not woodland. In the middle of Ashwell, Hertfordshire, the River Cam bursts from the ground in a great spring, to the Anglo-Saxons a 'well', beneath the roots of venerable ash trees. Was such a scene repeated in other 'ash' places? Were they so called because ash was abundant, or because they had the only ash tree for miles around? Was ash somehow a specially notable tree?

Irish place-names are very different. Oak and hawthorn are by far the commonest tree-elements, followed by yew. Ash appears in names like *Funshin*, from Old Irish *uinnius* 'ash'; it is in about eighth place, even though Ireland has more than its share of famous ash trees (*see* Table 2, pages 74–75). In Welsh place-names oak and alder are the commonest trees; ash (as in *Llwyn-On*, Grove-Ashes) comes well down the list.

Alphabetic ash

Æsc, Old English for Ash, is the name of the letter Æ and of its equivalent rune: ᚫ. The Anglo-Saxon runic alphabet began with ᚠ (F) for *Fee*, ᚢ (U) for *aUrochs*, ᚦ (TH) for *THorn…*, and letter 26 was ᚫ (*Æsc*) for Ash. Five of the 29 runic letters have the names of trees. (Scandinavian and Icelandic runes do not have this letter.) The *Runic Poem*, dating from the eighth to tenth century, copied before the original was consumed in the fire that destroyed the Cotton manuscripts in 1731, contained this unhelpful verse:

ᚫ   Ash is over-tall   dear to people
      Stiff on stem   stays erect on stool
      though against it fight   many men.

In the Irish Ogham alphabet *onn*, 'ash tree', is the name of the letter ᚘ, meaning O, but in another version the letter *nin* ᚅ, meaning N, is instead glossed as *uinnius,* 'ash tree'. The alphabet has 25 letters, of which in different versions between 7 and 17 have the names of trees.

Literary ash

It cannot be said that ash is a favourite or even much-noticed tree with poets, playwrights, and novelists. Tennyson was fonder of trees than most writers: he mentions pine 55 times and oak 54 times, but ash only 9 times. Easily available

Table 3 The more commonly-mentioned trees in the works of literary writers.

	Shakespeare	Wordsworth	Tennyson	Yeats
Oak	31	49	54	21
Pine	11	47	55	8
Yew	5	23	22	16
Willow	9	18	16	16
Hazel	3	6	9	35
Beech	0	10	14	22
Elm	3	22	21	4
Ash	**1**	**13**	**9**	**16**
Poplar	0	2	19	8
Cedar	11	6	10	1
Cypress	5	7	12	4
Holly	2	14	10	1
Birch	2	14	3	3
Lime, Linden	0	2	14	0

concordances reveal that Shakespeare was even less partial to ash, and Wordsworth not much more: only Yeats, as befits an Irishman, puts hazel at the top of the list and ash as high as fifth place.

Literary allusions to ash are tangential and seldom form a pattern. Maybe understanding and appreciating ash trees was a proletarian characteristic of people whose thoughts seldom reached print. John Clare loved ash trees but there seems to be no concordance to all his voluminous writings.

At the lowest level there are mere lists of tree names, not

revealing a real interest by the writer in how one tree differs from another. Virgil in the seventh *Eclogue* (first century BC) makes Thyrsis, his Arcadian shepherd, one of his most conventional characters, sing that ash (not necessarily our ash) was the most beautiful tree of woodland, like pine (which pine?) of gardens and poplar (which poplar?) of rivers.

Some poets notice the velvety-black buds of ash and its late leafing, as did Tennyson:

> More black than ash-buds
> in the front of March
>
> *Gardener's Daughter* (1842)

> Delaying, as the tender ash delays
> to clothe herself, when all the woods are green.
>
> *Princess* (1847)

Ash seldom inspires patriotism except in Kipling's merry 'A Tree Song':

> Of all the trees that grow so fair,
>   Old England to adorn,
> Greater is none beneath the sun,
>   Than Oak, and Ash, and Thorn.
> Sing Oak, and Ash, and Thorn, good sirs,
>   (All of a Midsummer morn!)
> Surely we sing of no little thing,
>   In Oak, and Ash, and Thorn!
>
> *Puck of Pook's Hill* (1906)

A consistent idea from Homer to Ovid to Beowulf to Sir Walter Scott to Yeats is that ash is the wood of warriors' and hunters' spears. In Old English the mere mention of *æsc*, 'ash', was supposed to be read as 'spear', much as cricket writers now say 'willow' meaning 'bat'. (But, lest interpretation be simple, *æsc* is also a metaphor for 'ship', although it is a most

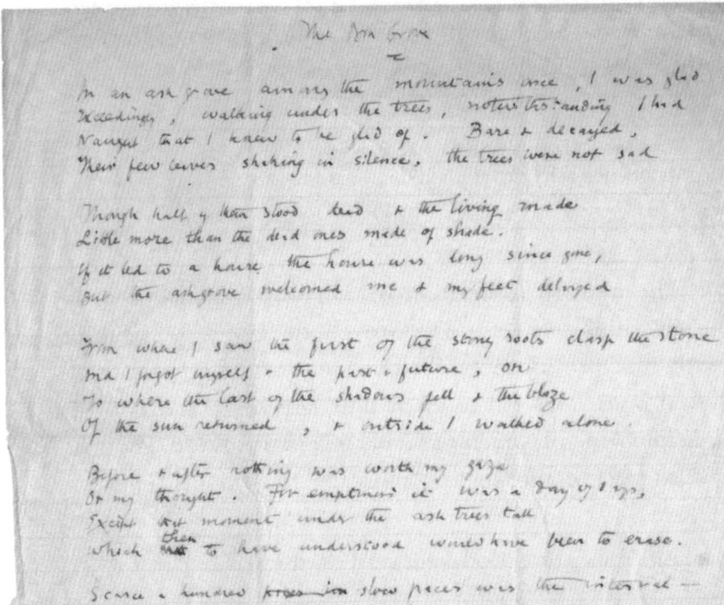

The Ash Grove

In an ash grove among the mountains once, I was glad
Exceedingly, walking under the trees, notwithstanding I had
Naught that I knew to be glad of. Bare & decayed,
Their few leaves shaking in silence, the trees were not sad

Though half of them stood dead & the living made
Little more than the dead ones made of shade.
If it led to a house the house was long since gone,
But the ashgrove welcomed me & my feet delayed

From where I saw the first of the stony roots clasp the stone
And I forgot myself & the past & future, on
To where the last of the shadows fell & the blaze
Of the sun returned, & outside I walked alone.

Before & after nothing was worth my gaze
Or my thought. For emptiness it was a day of days,
Except that moment under the ash trees tall
Which ~~that~~ then to have understood would have been to erase.

Scarce a hundred ~~paces~~ in slow paces was the interval —
Paces each sweeter than sweetest miles — but nothing at all,
Not even the spirits of memory & foreseeing,
Could climb in upon me over the wall

Till I passed through at either end without noticing.
And now an ash grove far from those hills can bring
The same tranquillity in which I wander a ghost
With a ghostly gladness, as if I heard a girl sing

The song of the Ash Grove soft as I love it most,
And then in a crowd or in distance it were lost,
But the moment gave it an immortality
As they did those trees, without search, or desert, or cost.

Fig. 46 Manuscript of 'The Ash Grove' by Edward Thomas, a poem written in February 1916.

unlikely timber for shipbuilding.) This 2,500-year-old cliché was repeated by Shakespeare in his only mention of the tree, as two old and friendly antagonists meet:

> . . . let me twine
> Mine arms about that body, wheregainst
> My grainèd ash one hundred times hath broke
> And scarr'd the moon with splinters . . .
>
> *Coriolanus*, IV.5.114

The modern association of ash with melancholy may begin with *Llwyn Onn* ('Ash Grove'), the famously beautiful early-nineteenth-century Welsh song lamenting the death of loved ones. This ran to many different Welsh and English versions, one of which probably inspired Edward Thomas, Welsh poet of the English landscape, to write his 'The Ash Grove':

> Half of the grove stood dead, and those that yet lived made
> Little more than the dead ones made of shade.
> If they led to a house, long before they had seen its fall . . .

Probably this was inspired by some desolation that he had seen in northern France, a few weeks before he himself was killed in the Battle of Arras in 1917.

Spiritual ash

Much has been written about veneration of trees and groves in the religions of prehistoric and early historic Britain and Ireland, but how much can one believe? Writers tend to confuse the religions of early prehistory: 'Celts' (as though Irish, British and Gauls were the same), Romans, Anglo-Saxons and Norsemen seem to merge; pagan theology is confused with the magic and medicine of much later ages

THE:ELDER:EDDA
COMMONLY CALLED
SÆMUND'S:EDDA:
EDITED:AND
TRANSLATED:BY
OLIVE:BRAY
PART:I

Fig. 47 W.G. Collingwood's title page for Oliver Bray's 1908 translation of the *Poetic Edda*. Yggdrasil is represented as a stylised but recognisable ash tree.

and the modern New Age revival. Sources are often not given, and where they can be traced tend to be from people who lived long after, had never seen, and were hostile to the practices involved. Archaeological evidence, especially for trees, is meagre.

However, ash has some claim to be more sacred than other trees in pre-Roman England. Its remains are the most often identified tree in what are regarded as votive deposits from Iron Age, but not Roman, times. Much later, the World Tree of the Norsemen, Yggdrasil, that upheld the world of gods, humanity and worms, is said to have been an ash – though that identification comes from the *Poetic Edda* written in the thirteenth century, by which time the old gods had long been demoted to heroes of romance.

Anglo-Saxon Christianity developed its own tree-symbolism: the Cross of Christ was thought of as a tree, though not, it seems, any particular kind of tree. Written allusions to actual sacred trees are few. The charters have half-a-dozen, for example 'crucifix oaks'. In the Taunton, Somerset, perambulation of 854 are four ash trees, one being 'an ash which the inexperienced call sacred'. Was this a lingering memory of one or other of the old religions? Or was it venerated by dissident Christians?

There might once have been sacred ashes in Christian churchyards, like the yews associated with Welsh saints. The walking sticks of a number of Anglo-Saxon saints are said to have grown into ash trees; but these would have died and disappeared centuries ago – unlike the long-lived yews that are still with us.

Ireland is different. The sacred and venerated trees are

hawthorn, ash and yew: seldom oak, although oak is by far the commonest in Irish place-names. In the earliest sources, going back to a dimly-remembered heroic past, ash is the commonest: thus of the five mighty legendary *bile* trees of ancient Ireland three were ash and two yew. Trees associated with saints tend to be hawthorn and a few ash. The many sacred trees of modern Ireland, especially those of holy wells, are about one-half hawthorn and one-third ash. (Ash is now probably the commonest non-woodland tree of Ireland.)

Ash timber crafts

Two Oxford dons, Helen Fitzrandolph and Doriel Hay, toured English factories and workshops in the 1920s to investigate the uses of different trees. Their book, *The Rural Industries of England and Wales* (1928), was followed after the Second World War by the forester Herbert Edlin's *Woodland Crafts in Britain* (1949). Although much has been written about woodland crafts since, these remain the definitive works. Both lack a time dimension: it is easy to suppose that the trades of the early- and mid-twentieth century were what was left of a timeless tradition of craftsmanship going back into a remote and unspecified past. This is no more likely to be so for wood than it would be for pottery. To some extent this lack has been remedied by the publication of Adam Bowett's magnificent books on furniture (*see* Bibliography), although inevitably he deals more with high-status work and says little about archaeological material.

John Evelyn, the seventeenth-century writer, had an enthusiasm for ash second only to his eloquence for oak:

The use of *Ash* is (next to that of the *Oak* it self) one of the most universal . . . The *Carpenter, Wheel-wright, Cart-wright, Cooper, Turner* and *Thatcher*: Nothing like it for our Garden *Palisad-hedges, Hop-yards, Poles* and *Spars, Handles, Stocks for Tools, Spade-trees*, &c. . . . *Carts, Ladders* and other tackling . . . the *white* and rotten dottard part composes a *ground* for our Gallants *Sweet-powder,** and the *Truncheons*** make the third sort of the most durable *Coal*† . . . the very *dead-leaves* afford (like those of the *Elm*) relief to our *Cattel* in *Winter*, but the shade of them is not to be endur'd, because it produces a noxious *Insect*††; and for displaying themselves so very *late*, and falling very *early*, not to be planted for *Umbrage*§, or *Ornament*; especially near the *Garden*; since (besides their predatitious *Roots*) the deciduous *leaves* descending with so long a *Stalk* are drawn by clusters into the *Worm-holes*, which foul the *Allies*§§ with their falling *Keys*, and suddenly infect the ground . . .

Sylva (1664)

* some masculine cosmetic
** unwanted short pieces of coppice-pole
† charcoal
†† not clear what this means
§ shade
§§ alleys, that is avenues

Much of this – even the sweet-powder – is borne out by later evidence, but definite evidence on the history of uses of trees is scattered in snippets among a thousand archaeological and ethnographic publications.

William Cobbett, enthusiastic follower of John Evelyn, declared:

We could not well have a wagon, a cart, a coach or a wheelbarrow, a plough, a harrow, a spade, an axe, or a hammer, if we had no Ash.

The Woodlands (1825)

Cobbett had not heard that in that very year his countrymen in Australia, where there was no ash nor anything like it, were busy finding alternative timbers.

I begin, like Helen Fitzrandolph and Doriel Hay, by separating timber and underwood industries. Some trades require ash to make use of its special properties; for others the species are more or less interchangeable, and ash is just a general-purpose tree.

In 2013, ash timber was offered by many dealers and cost less than oak, as it usually has done in the past. Much of it came from the Continent and even America. As with oak, 'high-quality' ash, which many estates seek to produce, is straight-grained, fast-grown, uniform in colour, without knots or black heart – a bland, plastic-like material, denying the irregularities that make ash and oak distinctive. (Is this an attempt to copy the bland qualities of American ash?)

Carpentry

Ash appears in some of the oldest surviving timber-framed buildings, but usually as a minor component of low-status structures, in places where oak or elm would have served as well. This was a means of using up ash trees and parts of them that were unsuitable for more specialised purposes. Occasionally, however, ash appears as a more substantial part of historic buildings, even in the Middle Ages.

Ash, a low-status material, seldom appears as ordinary timber in the building contracts which are the basis of L.F. Salzman's great book on medieval building history (*see* Bibliography). It was sometimes used for specialised purposes, such as scaffolding poles; in 1324, at Westminster, there was a remarkable order for 61 pieces of ash, 42 feet long, for scaffolding. Although the pegs of timber-framed buildings are oak, temporary pegs called *hokepynnes* were made of ash (like a modern tent peg, which is also made of ash, Fig. 51) and were sometimes used to hold joints loosely while the rest of the frame was assembled, and then replaced with oaken pegs.

Wheelwrighting and wainwrighting

Timber-framed wheels have an elm nave (hub), oak spokes, and a ring of curved ash felloes, one to every two spokes: thus a twelve-spoke wheel has six felloes. George Sturt's classic *The Wheelwright's Shop* (1923) describes how felloes were hewn out from quarter-logs while still green, left to season for months, and then worked to the final shape. The felloes took advantage of ash's resistance to being bent out of shape, either when the wheel was still and all the load came on the bottom felloe, or from the shocks and jolts when moving over an uneven road. Wheelwrights presumably would have had the first choice of suitable curved pieces whenever a batch of ash trees was felled. Alternatives were possible but rare: beech was occasionally used for wheels that were not protected by an iron rim.

This is a long-standing practice: the Tanworth-in-Arden estate in Warwickshire, inventory of *c.*1500 lists how many felloes each of the 594 hedgerow ash trees might provide. Much earlier still, the wheels of Iron Age chariot burials found in Yorkshire are said to have had ash naves as well as one-piece rings of ash bent into a circle (*see* p.56).

Allied is the use of ash for making the hoops of sieves. A thin ash plank would be bent into a circle, with a long, tapered overlap secured by bent-over nails. Tennis rackets are

Fig. 48 Wheelwright planing the ash ring of a seven-felloe wheel after assembly. Houghton, Stockbridge (Hants) *c.*1970.

made similarly, apart from the handle.

Wheelwrighting is related to *wainwrighting*, building vehicles. Ash, being resilient and capable of steam bending, was used for the shafts of horse-drawn carts and carriages, and for other components if the vehicle was kept under cover – but not much used for railway wagons that stood out in the rain. In the twentieth century, this expanded into timber-framed cars (like the Ford Woody and Morris Traveller), lorries and buses. Ash was used in wooden aircraft, later superseded by birch plywood, spruce and balsa wood.

Cabinet-making

Ash has been used sporadically in furniture. Loudon recommends it for kitchen tables because it can be scrubbed without running splinters into the fingers. It was preferred for contact with food before sycamore was available. In 1517, the infant Corpus Christi College, Oxford, purchased three ash planks, each 17 feet by 22 inches, for making a kneading-trough, pastry boards and college tables. They seem to have been unnecessarily large and expensive: they cost 18 pence each (about £60 in 2013 money).

Ash furniture is uncommon in early domestic inventories. It has occasionally been used for the visible parts of high-status furniture – even as a veneer hiding some lesser timber. I know a Suffolk house where a whole room is elaborately panelled in ash. American ash began to be imported in 1741, and was used especially for the interiors of expensive chests-of-drawers.

One specific use is chairs. The few surviving pre-1700 chairs tend to be high-status examples, especially those made of elaborately turned components (*spindles*) intended to display the wood-turner's virtuosity rather than to be sat on. Ash tends to be preferred because of its pretty grain. As the Windsor-type chair developed in the eighteenth century, the turned parts were often made of ash. The curved *bow* that surrounds the back is usually ash, steam-heated and bent. The seat is rarely ash, the more reliable elm being used instead. Later, as furniture-making became industrialised and concentrated in the beechwoods of the High Wycombe area, most of the components came to be made of beech (the last to go to beech being the seat).

A source of early wooden artefacts is the miscellany of objects that people in the seventeenth century used to hide around their chimney stacks, apparently as a precaution against sorcery. Among such a hoard at Crowfield in Suffolk I have seen chair legs turned from ash, probably a turner's rejects.

Although black heart is disapproved of, 'olive ash', with slight discoloration, has been regarded as decorative and a look-alike for the much more expensive olive. Evelyn said in 1679:

> Some ash is so curiously cambleted and veined, that skilful cabinet-makers prize it equally with ebony, and call it green ebony.

There was a minor fashion for ash furniture and ash-veneered furniture in the twentieth century. It went well with the now old-fashioned modernism of the 1960s, when shiny chromium-plated steel tubes were matched with wooden parts that imitated plastic imitations of wood.

Other timber crafts

Many tools and handles are made of ash coppice poles, but some are of timber, such as the D-shaped handle of a spade or fork, cut out of a single piece of ash (Fig. 49). An axe or adze helve is turned on a special lathe made to copy its three-dimensional shape. Small handles, except for hammers, are usually beech. In North America, hickory (a genus of trees related to walnut) is preferred to ash.

Oars are commonly ash, though the huge oars of Mediterranean galleys were normally beech, and the heavy oars of the Royal Navy were American ash. Medieval building contracts specify ash for replacing the helves, hafts and handles of masons' and carpenters' axes, mattocks, hammers, etc. Ash is recorded for hand-barrows and ladder rungs.

Ash continued to be used for turned wooden drinking vessels, especially cheap throwaway cups, for example the 800 'asshen cuppis' ordered for the Lord Mayor of London's feast in 1505.[1] Ash bark was of little value (though Loudon claimed it was used for tanning calf skins and fishing nets) and was often left on the timber.

Barrels, from the Middle Ages to the early twentieth century, were universal containers for everything from gunpowder to cement. For most liquids the staves had to be oak, but for 'dry cooperage' such as the herring trade they could be ash. The Crowfield chimney hoard in Suffolk included the head of a barrel, made of ash. Loudon says ash staves were used to make milk pails: they would avoid tainting the milk.

Ash underwood crafts

Many kinds of tools have been made of coppice poles. In the nineteenth century hundreds of small factories all over England made rakes, scythe handles, the robust shafts needed for pitchforks, and other ashen artefacts.

The Little Whelnetham Rake Factory near Bury St Edmunds, which operated into the 1970s, used ash from the Bradfield Woods (Fig. 51). Rake heads were sawn from big

1 Furnivall, F.J. (1908) *The Babees' Book: medieval manners for the young now first done into modern English,* Chatto & Windus.

Fig. 49 Twentieth-century tool handles, all made of ash.

Fig. 50 Bending cleft ash for tennis racket frames.
(From Edlin's *Woodland Crafts.*)

ash poles, planed and drilled in an automatic machine with holes to receive the split ends of the handle and the teeth. Rake teeth, split and then rounded by forcing them through a steel tube, were hammered into their holes without glue (broken teeth could thus be easily replaced) and pointed with a drawknife. Poles for rake handles were cut usually at 14 years' growth, heated in a steam chest to make them flexible, bent to perfect straightness, and trimmed to a slightly tapering cylinder in a mechanical lathe. For the *sneaths* of scythes with their three-dimensional curves, a pole would be shaved to a tapering shape, heated to make it flexible, and held down by hooks in a wooden *mould* so that as it cooled it would set in the curves needed for a scythe-stick. The two handles of a scythe were separately turned from short lengths of ash. For some uses ash was not essential: thus rake handles were sallow or birch, mop handles were alder, scythe-sticks could be birch instead of ash. Sometimes there would be a big order for ash tent pegs.

The Crowfield chimney hoard included an ash rake head, more elaborate than the Whelnetham kind, with ashen teeth.

Ash was used for hop poles, lasting a few years, when chestnut was not available.

Another ash underwood craft is hurdle-making. The familiar woven wattle hurdle is usually made of hazel or sallow, but there is a small proportion of ash in the very earliest example, the walkway known as the Sweet Track in Somerset, Neolithic of *c.*3800 BC (*see* Fig. 29, page 54). The other type of hurdle, like a small six- or seven-barred gate, the more familiar kind a century ago, can be made of ash, willow, or oak sapwood. The components are split from large

Fig. 51 Little Whelnetham Rake Factory, Suffolk, 1970, from top left to right: (**a**) Newly cut poles partly barked and set out for seasoning. (**b**) Bending handle-poles in a *brake* or *crotch*. The workman uses a draw-knife to take bark off the inside of the next bend. (**c**) Spokeshave, for use by hand. The stock of the tool is beech. (**d**) Inserting teeth in a rake-head. The pot contains water. Ashen tent pegs behind. (**e**) Power-driven shave for tapering scythe-sticks. The stock is elm. (**f**) Bending scythe-sticks in the mould to the correct curve. The one in the foreground is completed and has its handles attached.

coppice poles, morticed where the uprights receive the rails, and fastened with nails (Fig. 52).

Ash poles were one of the materials for barrel hoops before steel hoops became universal. They were made in vast numbers, and the many people named Hooper commemorate this craft. The poles were split and bent in various ways, either cold or hot, the overlap being secured with a rivet. The bark was usually left on, which was a disadvantage because the ash bark beetle would bore into the hoop. Ash crates used to be used for packing pottery; this went on until they were banned in a fit of concern about biosecurity, lest they introduce ash bark beetles to countries that had ash trees but not the beetles.

Ash was one of many woods used to make particular types of arrow, as in the *Mary Rose* shipwreck. It was not normally used for bows, although regulations for bow-sellers in 1565 mention it is as a possible wood.[2] Ash is the traditional, as well as proverbial, material for military spears, although the massive lightweight jousting lances in the Tower of London appear to be pine.

Ash is still the material for most kinds of sporting bats for hitting a hard ball (except cricket bats): hurling sticks, shinty sticks, hockey sticks and (in America) baseball bats. It is also said to be the material of policemen's truncheons. A minor use for one-year ash coppice rods was as a teaching aid – and, it was alleged, for beating wives.

Ash is ring-porous: the row of big vessels at the start of each annual ring forms a plane of weakness. Hammering a piece of slow-grown ash will split the big vessels and allow

2 Statute: 8 Elizabeth c.10.

Fig. 52 Nailing diagonal struts to cleft ash hurdle, Essex, *c.*1949.

the annual rings to be separated as a bundle of flexible laths. In Central Europe these are woven into baskets, and bent into circles to form the walls of round boxes and box lids. This craft was practised from the Bronze Age until now. As far as I know, the only equivalent in Britain was the strange art of making *laps* or ties to hold birch brooms together. One of the many ways of doing this was to take an ash log and hammer it all round until the outer layer of wood was reduced to fibres which could be used like twine.

In Fitzrandolph and Hay's time, an 'odd art' was making walking sticks out of small ash trees. A stick was as essential an accessory for an able-bodied, respectable man as a handbag is for women today. Fashion then required that the handle make an abrupt angle with the stick, which could only be achieved by specially training the ashling to include part of the root as the handle.

Ash has a supreme, perhaps undeserved, reputation as firewood. This is somewhat surprising, since ash contains no resin and when standing, alive or dead, is impossible to burn. It seems to be derived from a literary source, 'The Firewood Poem', written in the 1920s by Celia Congreve. It sets out the virtues of various species:

> Elm wood burns like churchyard mould,
> E'en the very flames are cold.
> But ash green or ash brown
> Is fit for a queen with golden crown.
>
> .   .   .
>
> . . . ash wet or ash dry
> a king shall warm his slippers by.

I cannot agree with Lady Congreve: ash (when well dried) is much better than light woods like alder and sallow, but roughly equivalent to maple and elm of similar density. Its rather low moisture content would be an advantage, but maybe in a damp and draughty palace it is the best a sovereign can get.

Uses of ash leaves

Leafy twigs of ash, dried like hay, have been used for feeding livestock when grass is not growing, as they still are in the Alps and Scandinavia (Fig. 53). This was one of the reasons for pollarding ash and goes back to Neolithic times. This practice probably declined when the iron scythe made it possible to mow and dry grass.

Fig. 53 Pollard ashes, the arisings from which are used as an alternative to hay. Ire, Blekinge, Sweden, September 2000.

Loudon in 1838 says that ash leaves were used to feed cattle in autumn or spring and for adulterating tea. There are twenty-first-century recipes for ash keys pickled in vinegar, but I hesitate to recommend them, dear reader, as I am yet to taste this delicacy myself.

Ash in art

Depicting a convincing bare tree is the most difficult task of the artist, except for depicting a convincing leafy tree. No painting, drawing or photograph of a big tree can be naturalistic: life isn't long enough to paint all the details. This means any picture is a caricature, picking out those details that are significant, which very few artists have known how to do. Ash might be easier than most, because its coarse twig structure means that less detail has to be discarded; but I have seen few convincing pictures of whole ash trees, even pollards which should be more distinctive.

John Constable admired trees with 'an ecstasy of delight', according to his biographer. 'The ash was his favourite, and all who are acquainted with his pictures cannot fail to have observed how frequently it is introduced as a near object.'[3] But did he really draw a recognisable ash? Not obviously in his paintings, but there are several sketches under the title of ash trees – some represent the same tree, and one of the few identifiable is really a white poplar. (Constable himself was not always responsible for the titles of his works.)

David Hockney's pictures sometimes portray the empty repetitiveness of planted trees, but he also comes near to bringing out the character of a gnarled veteran ash in a hedge. Then there is David Nash – whose very name apparently comes from 'at aN ASH' – who in 1977 planted *Ash Dome* near his home in Wales as a living work of art:

> My main source for research into which species of tree to use was hedgerows. I noticed that ash was resilient and vigorous and recovered most readily from being pruned or fletched. And in woods I observed that ash trees could lean a long way from their roots in search of light.

Forty years on, he still maintains the *Dome* using hedging methods (Fig. 55).

---

3 C.R. Leslie (1896) *Life and Letters of John Constable*, Chapman & Hall

Fig. 54 A John Constable ash sketch, titled by him as 'Hampstead June 21. 1823. Longest day, 9'o clock. Evening. Ash'. But is it recognisable as an ash tree? This shows how hard it is for even the most accomplished artists to draw a recognisable tree.

Fig. 55 The growth of David Nash's *Ash Dome* recorded in this pastel drawing by the artist in 1995.

Sculptors have used many timbers, from poplar (easily carved but not durable) to lime to fast-grown oak (durable, defeating all but the sharpest of tools) – or conifers in Japan. Ash, hard and perishable, was rarely used until Nash made it one of his favourite sculptural materials.

Medicinal ash

Ash seems not to be much used in historic 'official' medicine. The Anglo-Saxon *Leechdoms* is a strange compilation based on trying to identify the herbs recommended by Greek and Roman medicinal writers far away and centuries before. It recommends ash bark, mixed with many other substances, as a drug for human complaints ranging from leprosy to stroke to 'wormeating'. Herbals recite a similarly random assortment of minor virtues. In Roman times, Pliny and Dioscorides had written of ash as repelling serpents and curing serpent bite. This was repeated in the thirteenth century (although the kind of ash and the kind of snake were both different by then), when Bartholomew the Englishman said in his encyclopædia 'If a serpent be set between a fire and ash leaves he will flee into the fire.' Later still, this 'property' of ash was repeated in Gerard's *Herball* (1597).

The *London Pharmacopœia*, first published in 1618, has on its list ash roots, bark of ash roots, ash leaves and ash seeds, but without saying what they were used for. They rarely, if ever, appear among the complex pills and potions that fill the book. John Hall, Shakespeare's doctor-relative, prescribed ash bark only three times among his recorded cases. He used it to make medicated beer or wine: each time it was one of about 30 ingredients. Even in 1900 the *United States Pharmacopœia* ascribed vague virtues ('tonic and astringent') to ash bark.

In Loudon's time ash seeds were prescribed for common complaints like dropsy and stone. The sap that comes out of a fresh 'truncheon' of ash when one end is heated was given to newborn babies, or used to treat earache, or, as a French doctor recommended, 'is an excellent remedy for the gangrene', no less.

Manna is a sugary product containing the sugar called *mannose*, tapped from the manna ash (*Fraxinus ornus*) of southern Europe. English ash also yields a sugary sap (which I have once seen dribbling from the tree), although it is less effective than maple or birch, let alone American sugar maple.

Magical ash

Magic is often interpreted as a vestige of one or other of the old religions, or a misinterpretation of Christianity. Although some spells appealed to saints or heathen gods, most magic is an affair of this world, pseudo-science rather than pseudo-theology. If your cow suffers from having had a shrew run over her and you rub the sore place with a twig from a shrew-ash tree, she will get better. If you put deadly nightshade in your enemy's fruit salad, he will die. Neither treatment appeals to the supernatural, and both are likely to work.

In the context of magical attributions in modern folklore (mostly from works published between 1850 and 1930) Ronald Hutton finds:

> All over northern Europe [ash] was regarded as the most arcane of trees, and there are more superstitions recorded about it in folklore collections from the British Isles than any other species.

However, other authors, such as Sir James Frazer in *The Golden Bough*, report less about ash than yew or rowan, which were much less common trees at the time. Richard Mabey says little about ash, apart from some minor schoolchildren's games and rituals, like 'mud yacks'.

Roy Vickery, an authority on early- and late-modern plant lore, says more about ash than any tree except horsechestnut, but most of it is lightweight – like the parades of ash twigs on

Fig. 56 'Bid my true love come to me, Between moonlight and firelight, Bring him over the hill tonight.' Perhaps this ash charm from the New Forest, Hampshire, helped a young woman to find a husband. From the Museum of Witchcraft, Boscastle, Cornwall.

Ash Wednesday, presumably because of a false connection between ash and Ash. Much of his material is from in or around Somerset, like the mentions of ash in Anglo-Saxon charters a thousand years before (*see* p.57).

Failure of ash to set seed was an omen portending the fall of kings, like Charles I. Ash was one of the trees put under their pillows by girls to identify their future husbands. Burning the Ash Faggot was – maybe still is – an alternative to a Yule Log at Christmas.

The various 'oak before ash' proverbs seem to be examples of proverbial tautology. Has anyone seen ash leaf before oak? In 50 years I never have, and only twice have they come into leaf simultaneously.

Fig. 57 Ancient shrew-ash, Richmond Park, in 1903.

Gilbert White, the great eighteenth-century naturalist, mentions two famous examples that all writers quote. He knew 'rupture-ashes' that had been used to treat infants' hernias by splitting the tree, passing the patient through the split, and binding up and plastering the tree. 'If the parts coalesced and soldered together, as usually fell out where the feat was performed with any adroitness at all, the party was cured.' This was practised, with ritual variations, for treating hernia, rickets, and occasionally impotence, in many parts of England, and last heard of in the 1880s – always with ash, although elsewhere in Europe other trees might be used. It was advisable to preserve the tree throughout the patient's life, for if it were cut down the rupture would return and kill the person, 'be the patient ever so distant' – although it was not uncommon 'for persons to survive for a time the felling of the tree'.

White's veterinary example concerned an ill-defined disease of cattle attributed to shrews running over them. A hole was bored in an ash tree and a live shrew walled up in it. Ever after, 'the tree was looked on with no small veneration as a shrew-ash'. Branches cut from the tree would be used to treat affected animals. An ancient pollard shrew-ash was pointed out and photographed in Richmond Park all through the nineteenth century: its virtue extended to human ailments like whooping-cough that had nothing to do with shrews. Writers such as White held up both practices as examples of 'superstition', although they were probably no less effective than the mainstream medical procedures of the time.

None of the 'real' magic attached to ash trees lives up to the literary magic in M.R. James's *The Ash Tree*. James, Cambridge don and supreme writer of ghost stories, creeps the reader's flesh with the great ash tree that grew too near a bedroom window of the Hall. . . the moonlight visits of Mrs Mothersole, the last witch to be hanged. . . the squirrel with too many legs for a squirrel. . . the Squires who rarely slept in that room and when they did never woke up. . . the tree that [un-ash-like] burst into flames. . . and the Things that came out of that tree as it burnt. . . Brrr!!

5 Pests and Diseases

> Once is happenstance.
> Twice is coincidence.
> Three times, it's enemy action.
>
> IAN FLEMING, *Goldfinger*, 1956

Ash and deer

IN BRITAIN THERE ARE MORE DEER than at any time for a thousand years, and more deer species – red, roe, fallow, muntjac, Japanese (sika) and Chinese water deer – than ever in history or prehistory. Until a century ago deer were relatively rare, largely confined to parks and royal Forests. The sudden change from little browsing to an unprecedented level of browsing, which is not part of the normal dynamics of woodland, has had a huge impact. Not only in Britain: too many deer threaten trees and forests worldwide, especially in countries like New Zealand that never had deer.

Red and roe deer are native. Fallow deer, originally from south-west Asia, were introduced by the Normans 900 years ago, and became the chief deer of deer-parks and Forests like Epping Forest. They did not normally spread into ordinary woodland until the mid-twentieth century. Then they were joined by three other species, all brought from the Far East and escaping from parks.

In 1964, what is now Cambridgeshire Wildlife Trust, having acquired Hayley Wood, resumed coppicing on 14 one-acre plots. Regrowth, especially of ash, failed, which was at first

Fig. 58 Deer are not fools. They know that a plastic tree guard means dinner inside.

attributed to the long gap since the previous coppicing, 38 or 66 years before. Experimental fences established that this was not so: regrowth was being eaten by fallow deer that had colonised the wood in the interval. Ash was the second most palatable species, after elm. With few exceptions, the big old ash stools failed to recover and have now disappeared – until, in the later plots, pollarding was tried instead of coppicing.

In some plots there was a dense crop of new ash seedlings, which (if they got past the first year) the deer nibbled but did not kill. When these plots were fenced in 1980 the gnarled ashlings shot up into young trees, which were coppiced for the first time when their turn came. The result is a dense stand of small ash stools which have now been cut twice or three

Fig. 59 Ashwood, severely browsed by three species of deer. Note absence of herbaceous plants (except distasteful dog's mercury) and absence of low cover. Hempstead Wood, Essex, April 2002.

Fig. 60 Ash regrowth in Hayley Wood, July 1973, stops six inches inside a deer exclosure. Fallow deer have poked their noses through the fence as far as they can reach.

times. I hesitate to say that intermittent browsing encourages ash, for on other plots this has not happened and the stand is now dominated by hazel, which recovers after browsing.

Deer tend to live in woods and eat all edible vegetation within reach. When that has gone they go out and eat the surrounding fields. Deer-ravaged woods are now all too familiar: a wood in which the tree and shrub foliage stops suddenly at the height that deer can reach; coppiced areas fail unless fenced; there are no young trees; woodland herbaceous plants are replaced by grasses or a few unpalatable species (Fig. 59). Such a wood has a dubious future.

I have discussed mainly fallow deer. Roe deer have similar tastes but do not form herds and are not quite so damaging. The commonest deer are now muntjac, small and non-gregarious. It is impracticable to eliminate muntjac from Hayley Wood; damage to ash is noticeable but far less than from fallow. In Monks Wood, Huntingdonshire, muntjac alone have done vast damage to trees (especially ash and hazel) and herbaceous plants. Coppicing had to be suspended because fencing against muntjac was ineffective. However, muntjac were exceptionally abundant there: an observer would see 15–20 per hour instead of the usual two or three per day.

Caterpillar defoliation

Plagues of caterpillars, especially tortrix moths, sometimes devour leaves after they emerge on the trees, especially in the oak-dominated woods of north and west England and Wales.

There was an instance, so far unique, in Hayley Wood in June 1980. Caterpillars defoliated oak, ash, hazel, maple and aspen, canopy trees and coppice shoots, almost impartially, though some areas were more affected than others. Some trees were leafless as in winter, but replaced the lost foliage within weeks. Ashes often lost the terminal buds, their replacements giving a bunched-foliage effect, but the incident left no permanent mark.

Ash canker and ash gall

Woodland ashes often display irregular warts, excrescences, and cavities on twigs, branches and trunks. They may range from irregular masses of tissue that replace the flowers to classic cankers on the trunk, with concentric growth-rings like the zones of an archery target. These seem not greatly to affect the tree, though the bigger cankers spoil the timber value and render a young tree unsightly and an old tree picturesque.

Ash canker, the larger lesions, seems not to be an introduced condition. This is a difficult disease to pin down. In nineteenth-century Cheshire, as Sir George Frazer the anthropologist claimed, it was caught from human beings, who would 'transfer' their warts to the tree by rubbing the place with a rasher of bacon and inserting the bacon

Fig. 61 Many ash flowers are turned into galls by a minute gall wasp. Hayley Wood, July 2013.

under the bark of an ash tree. Any connection with the human verruca virus has not been pursued more recently; such simple explanations are frustrated by the menagerie of miscellaneous bacteria and fungi inside well-developed cankers.

The primary cause appears to be a bacterium, *Pseudomonas savastanoi*, one of a group of bacteria that attack anything from horsechestnut to tomato. Another causes poplar canker, a major disease when poplars were grown commercially. The bacteria seem to aggravate frost damage, and when floating in the air have been credited with magicking raindrops into hailstones. *P. savastanoi* begins at a leaf or twig scar and starts a canker, which then is invaded by the fungus *Nectria galligena* and many other organisms. Cankers are systemic: one individual ash tree will be full of lesions, while its neighbours are exempt.

Ash flowers are attacked by a gall mite, *Aceria fraxinivora* (*Eriophyes fraxini*), which hijack the male flower's hormones and turn it into a welter of abortive twiglets (Fig. 61).

Ash rust

Ash Rust is an American ash disease with an alternation of generations. To complete its life cycle it needs cord-grass, the saltmarsh grass *Spartina alterniflora*. In North America it is widespread on ash trees near saltmarshes, doing minor damage to the tree.

Ash rust has not yet been found in Europe – 150 years ago its scope would have been limited by the distribution of native cord-grasses. But someone introduced American cord-grass to Britain, and *c.*1870 it hybridised with a native cord-grass and doubled its chromosomes to make a new and aggressive species, *Spartina × townsendii*, now more widespread than its forebears. What would happen if ever ash rust came into contact with this new creation remains to be seen.

Ash bark beetle

Under the bark of recently felled ash are the breeding galleries of small beetles, *Hylesinus*. The mother beetle makes a Y-shaped tunnel between bark and wood and lays eggs at intervals along it (Fig. 62). The eggs hatch and the grubs bore little tunnels of their own, diverging from the brood tunnel and getting gradually bigger as the grubs get fatter, until they pupate, turn into beetles, bore their way out, and fly away. There are four species, specialising in different sizes of ash;

Fig. 62 Breeding galleries of an ash bark beetle, *Hylesinus varius*.

they attack other ash species and even olive. The beetles have been here for at least 600 years (*see* Fig. 34, page 62).

Ash bark beetle resembles the elm bark beetles that transmit Elm Disease. It is unlikely to transmit Ash Disease. It attacks mainly felled logs and dead branches: it does little harm to the tree but may be a vector of ash canker.

Ash Disease

This book is a response to the eruption of public interest in ash in October 2012, following the announcement of a 'new' and 'terrible' disease. The disease was not very new: it should have been seen coming for 20 years. International conferences had been held on Ash Disease, at which Britain was absent.[1] What I say will soon be superseded by fresh developments.

Ash Disease is caused by the microscopic fungus *Chalara fraxinea,* which I have not seen (Fig. 64). It inhabits leaves and twigs, which it damages by making a chemical called *viridiol* that is very toxic to ash. In summer it attacks leaves and produces spores called *conidia*, which form sticky masses and may be spread around the tree by rain to start more infections (Fig. 63).

The fungus has an alternation of generations, as do many parasites (such as the tapeworm that people got from eating underdone pork). In autumn it turns into *Hymenoscyphus pseudoalbidus*, a white cup-fungus about 3 mm across, which appears on the fallen rhachis (midrib) of ash leaves, that falls

1 Much of what I say comes from the proceedings of a conference in Oslo in 2010.

separately from the leaflets (Fig. 65). Like the morels and *Pezizas* to which it is related, the cups puff out little clouds of *ascospores*. The ascospores measure about 17 x 4 μ (1 μ = 1/1000 mm); a single midrib may bear 20 cup-fungi, each producing 1,500 ascospores an hour for about two weeks: several million spores from each ash leaf. These dust-like spores float in the air, are blown by the wind and are thought to start infections in distant trees. When new leaves appear the fungus reverts to *Chalara* and continues the cycle.

Symptoms

Infected leaflets develop blackish spots. The whole leaf wilts, turns dark brown, withers and goes rigid, hanging down on the tree (Fig. 63a and 63b). The infection spreads into the twig as a slightly sunken bluish-black area, often confined to one side of the twig. An infection in a minor twig may continue into the branch. From the point of entry a long narrow strip of bark goes blackish and sunken and dies. The surrounding tissue is stimulated into callus growth, resulting in an elongated canker.

The progress of the fungus is contained and walled off by the tree's damage-limitation reaction (*see* p.66). The wood of an infected branch is discoloured brownish, extending downwards and sideways until it is delimited by a compartment boundary formed by the tree. Infections appear not to continue into subsequent years' growth (Fig. 67).

The tree next responds by producing new shoots from buds below the dead part. These can reach 8 ft long in one season (Fig. 66). In less vigorous trees the new shoots may be infected in turn, giving rise to bunched clusters of shoots

Fig. 63 Successive stages of Ash Disease. **(a)** Blackish spots appear on the leaflets and the leaf wilts. **(b)** Leaf withers and hangs rigidly. **(c)** Early stage of canker formation: sunken, blackish strip of bark extends up and down from a dead twig. **(d)** Stabilised canker: the dead strip (with remains of two dead twigs) is isolated by probably two years' growth of callus. East Suffolk, August 2013.

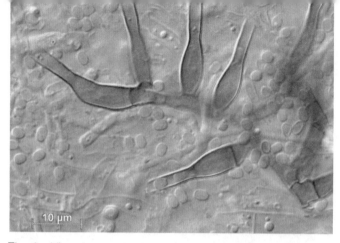

Fig. 64 The microscopic *Chalara fraxinea* fungus, that lives on leaves and twigs of ash trees and poisons them with viridiol. After Jankovsky & Holdenrieder.

like little witches'-brooms (Fig. 69). Eventually the whole tree may die.

Ash Disease is recognisable by four characteristics: wilted, rigid, blackish-brown leaves; a blackish strip of bark spreading up and down the twig; long narrow cankers with a dead twig in the middle; regrowth shoots leading to bunched foliage. These are not absolutely diagnostic: newly emerged leaves can be blackened by late frost, cankers can be the early stage of Ash Canker, bunched foliage is a common reaction to drought, and there are doubtless many other ash pathogens. Ash Disease is easily identified in young trees and coppice shoots. Middle-aged and old trees seem to be less easily infected; infections are difficult to detect at first, becoming evident when there are multiple dead twigs and bunched regrowth shoots.

The history of the disease can be estimated from the degree of branching of regrowth shoots, or if a stem cankered in

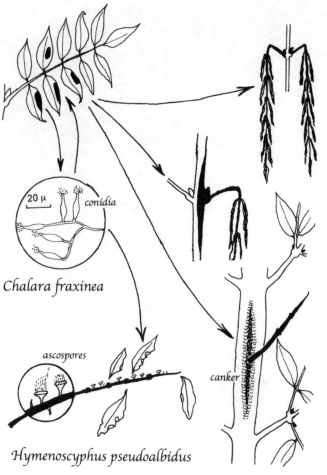

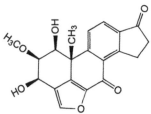

Fig. 65 Alternation of generations between *Hymenoscyphus* and *Chalara*, and the chemical structure of the deadly viridiol.

Fig. 66 *Chalara* attack over four years, as modified by pruning. The leading shoot was killed and was pruned away, along with some of the side branches, before *Chalara* had been identified in Britain. East Suffolk, August 2013.

Fig. 67 Anatomy of successive attacks. Discoloured wood marks the boundaries at which the infection was arrested by the tree's compartmentation mechanism.

Fig. 68 *Chalara* in a big ash tree, showing many dead twigs and a tendency to bunched foliage. Great Glemham, Suffolk, August 2013.

one year is killed by a more extensive infection in a later year. Another clue is from the growth of *Xanthoria* and other lichens on killed branches. Infections in 2011 and sometimes in 2010 can thus be identified in 2013; but where infections have been repeated in subsequent years the evidence is soon confused.

Chalara does not always (or usually?) kill the tree. Finnish and Czech scholars show infected ashes getting better as well as worse from year to year, but remark 'overall development negative'. In May 2012 I was on the Estonian island of Saaremaa, where disease had been present for many years. More than half the ash trees showed symptoms, but not many were dead (Fig. 69). I understand that there are many left alive in Poland after at least 22 years. However, a research article has already been inspired by the ecological effects of ash decline in Lithuania.

Fig. 69 In the island of Saaremaa, Estonia, where Ash Disease has been known for at least 20 years, most ash trees are infected but still alive. They are characterised by peripheral dieback and by a proliferation of shoots like little witches'-brooms. May 2012.

The two cup-fungi

Ash Disease was first noticed in or around Latvia *c.*1990, and has apparently spread across Europe from there. *Chalara* was published as a fungus new to science in 2006. In 2009 it was linked to the cup-fungus stage, interpreted as an obscure fungus called *Hymenoscyphus albidus*, known for over a century as inhabiting fallen ash leaves (Fig. 70). In 2010 Swiss investigators discovered that *Chalara* was really the pathogenic phase of a previously unrecognised cup-fungus, now named *Hymenoscyphus pseudoalbidus*. This is identical to *H. albidus* to look at but is genetically different, and may not even

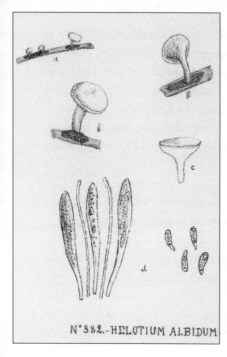

Fig. 70 The cup-fungus lookalike *H. albidus*, from Patouillard's original publication in 1882.

Fig. 71 Probably another lookalike: a cup-fungus on ash leaflets instead of the rhachis which is the normal habitat of *H. pseudoalbidus*. Bradfield Woods, Suffolk, November 2013.

be closely related. It can be told apart only by its DNA and because it can make the ash-damaging viridiol. *H. pseudoalbidus* cup-fungi are reported to appear in vast numbers on the Continent where *Chalara* disease has been active. They seem not to have been identified in Britain at the time of writing. I have not yet definitely seen *albidus* or *pseudoalbidus* cup-fungi, which appear to be among several lookalike species (Fig. 71) found on various kinds of fallen leaves.

H. pseudoalbidus could be an introduction to Europe, possibly from China or Japan, or it could be a new mutation or hybridisation from an existing fungus. More investigation is needed of *H. albidus*, the harmless variant, which in most accounts (including the original publication by Narcisse Théophile Patouillard *c.*1882) is produced on blackened patches of fallen ash-leaf stalks. Does it merely live on dead ash leaves? Does it have a *Chalara* stage, perhaps as a harmless endophyte permanently living inside its host? Does it produce small amounts of viridiol, causing fallen ash leaves to blacken?

According to the British Mycological Society's database, what is now called *H. albidus* was first definitely recognised in Britain by Ted Ellis, my old friend and teacher and specialist in tiny fungi, at Surlingham in Norfolk in 1940. Between then and 2010 there have been 127 records on ash, apparently getting more frequent, although this may reflect a growing interest in obscure cup-fungi. These would include any observations of *H. pseudoalbidus* had it been present. Their distribution, unlike either of the present distributions of *Chalara*, is concentrated around Worcestershire and Warwickshire. This, however, probably reflects the habits of those few people capable of recognising *Hymenoscyphus*. It is usually reported on the 'petiole' (leaf-stalk) of fallen ash leaves, perhaps in mistake for the 'rhachis' (midrib).

Ash Disease in Britain and Ireland

In 2009, the Horticultural Trades Association, representing responsible nurserymen, warned the Forestry Commission about the threat of Ash Disease; the Commission cited excellent legalistic reasons for doing nothing. Not until Ash Disease was noticed in England itself did the Forestry Commission react with belated promptitude. A great survey

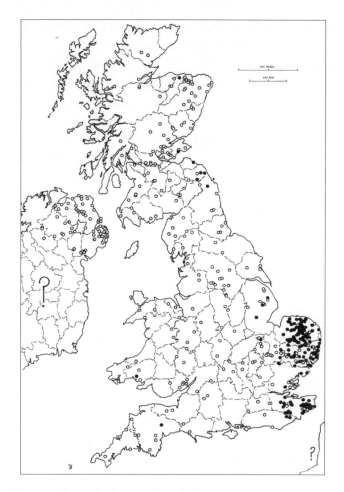

Fig. 72 Map of places where Ash Disease (or, rather, DNA indistinguishable from that of *Hymenoscyphus pseudoalbidus*) has been found, July 2013. White spots: recent plantings of ash trees. Black spots: not associated with recent planting. (No, the fungus doesn't really stop at the Irish border, but the surveyors did.) After map issued by DEFRA, by permission.

was got up, aided by new technology for rapidly matching the DNA of samples and thus distinguishing Ash Disease from similar but unrelated conditions. This revealed that *H. pseudoalbidus* was already present throughout Britain and Northern Ireland. Because of bureaucratic parochialism the survey was not continued into the rest of Ireland, although the fungus was there too.

By July 2013 the fungus – or, rather, something with DNA indistinguishable from that of the fungus – had been found in 549 sites. Of these, 24 were tree nurseries, 336 were in 'recently planted' ash (how recently is not stated), and 189 were in established ash trees in woods and in non-woodland sites. These have very different distributions (Fig. 72). Recent plantings were randomly scattered through the area surveyed. Finds in established trees were concentrated in East Anglia and Kent, with a few near the east coast into Scotland. Some of these were in ancient woodland, where ash shoots coppiced two to four years ago seemed to attract the disease.

A simple explanation is that nurseries inadvertently imported infected plants from the Continent and spread them all over Great Britain and (at least Northern) Ireland; this agrees with reports of nurseries spreading the disease in other countries. The tree-planting fashion has brought Ash Disease throughout England, far into Wales and the Scottish Highlands, and very efficiently into Ireland.

In contrast, disease in established ashes may represent infection spreading independently across the North Sea, possibly by windborne ascospores. But here I remember what Denis Garrett, plant pathologist, taught me 55 years ago. Whether an infection gets established depends on the *inoculum potential*: on the amount and condition of the infective material. A single minute ascospore, dried up by a long windborne journey, would hardly be capable of starting a new infection. More likely might be a mass of conidia stuck to the foot of a migrating bird. However, the fungus may have been here for many years without doing noticeable damage.

The Forestry Commission survey began in November 2012, when Ash Disease could still be seen in coppice shoots or planted ashes that still kept their leaves, but was difficult to spot in big trees that had shed their leaves earlier. I was told that what was being looked for was not the disease but the fungus, or rather something whose DNA is indistinguishable from that of *H. pseudoalbidus*. When the investigators could not find visible disease they sampled healthy ash trees. Thus Bradfield Woods, west Suffolk, appeared on the map before any disease had yet been found there.[2] In medical terms this is a *false positive*. I cannot say how many false positives there are – they were not separately mapped – but the fact that there are any indicates that the link between fungal DNA and disease is not simple. The Swiss investigators who first separated *pseudoalbidus* from *albidus* found that although most of their cup-fungi that had *pseudoalbidus* DNA were collected after Ash Disease was first noticed in Switzerland in 2007, two specimens dated from 1978 and 1987.

What do false positives mean? Is the DNA test not sensitive enough to be certain of separating *pseudoalbidus* from *albidus*? Or is *pseudoalbidus* everywhere, but some outside factor is needed to get it to switch on the genes that

2   This I have from Peter Fordham MBE, who has an intimate knowledge of the woods.

make the viridiol which poisons the host? These questions are not yet resolved.

The present position (early 2014)

Ash Disease is still not abundant: even in East Anglia one can travel a whole day and not notice it. My own experience is limited to half-a-dozen sites. Ash Disease is gregarious: there are clusters of thousands of infected trees, with few or none between.

I have seen four large-scale infections, three of which (A, B, C) are in 'recently-planted sites', planted 12–15 years ago, but one (site D) is in a very dense stand of young ash that was not planted (*see* p. 41). In three cases the disease is confined to these young trees and has not spread into big ashes in adjacent hedges or woodland; in site C, however, it has attacked big ash trees in a small wood in the middle of the planted area.

In all four places the disease did conspicuous damage in 2012 (Fig. 73), though without killing any trees except some that were suppressed and would have died anyway. Damage was not repeated in 2013, when there were comparatively few new or continuing infections. Instead, the trees produced vigorous replacement shoots from below the limit of the infection, which were seldom reinfected. Sometimes regrowth could be detected from an attack in 2011 and occasionally in 2010, but in young trees the evidence soon fades into obscurity.

In general, 2012 was an aggressive year and 2013 was not: this may have had some cause in the weather, such as the wet summer of 2012 or the drought of 2013. On the Forestry Commission's maps of *Chalara*, relatively few new localities

Fig. 73 Ash Disease in newly coppiced ash in 2012. Dramatic outbreaks such as this drew attention to the disease in England. In 2013 it was much less conspicuous.

were added in 2013, although this could represent waning efforts in finding them rather than decreasing rate of spread.

Experience in 2013 bears out the interpretation that Ash Disease has been distributed over the country on planted ash trees, probably since the late 1990s, and has lurked unnoticed until something caused it to flare up in 2012. This cannot be the whole story, since some outbreaks have nothing to do with planting. If, additionally, the disease drifted across the North Sea on wind or birds' feet, this might explain the eastern distribution of sites not linked to planting, but does not explain the clustered nature of such attacks. For example, the abundant disease in site D must represent a build-up over many years from an initial infection, during which time the disease should have spread over the surrounding countryside, but did not.

There are other possibilities. *Chalara* seems to be especially attracted to young trees and coppice shoots. Is it present all the time, but does some factor such as transplanting or coppicing cause it to switch on the genes that produce the viridiol that poisons the tree?

Chalara must have been present well before it attracted attention in 2012. It could easily pass unnoticed if high in a tree or not close to a path, or be mistaken for something else such as frost damage. Whether it is spreading and how rapidly is impossible to say, since reports do not distinguish between new attacks and newly-discovered old attacks. Will subsequent years be like 2012? Or like 2013, when ash trees appeared to be gaining on *Chalara* damage?

Emerald Ash Borer

This is 'one of the most feared beetles on earth', but not in these islands, where British parochialism ignores pests and diseases until they have got here and the battle to contain them has been lost.

Agrilus planipennis, a pretty little insect, about 8 mm long and iridescent green, is said to come from the Far East and to have got into North America in a shipment of Japanese car parts. It is a bark beetle: it lays its eggs on the tree; the grubs tunnel prodigiously between bark and wood, killing the tree (Fig. 74).

Fig. 74 'One of the most feared beetles on earth': the Emerald Ash Borer is busy exterminating ash across the United States. The grubs make multiple tunnels through the phloem (*right*), killing the tree at least to ground level. The emerging beetle leaves the tree through a D-shaped exit hole (*above*).

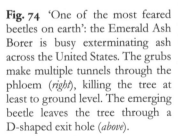

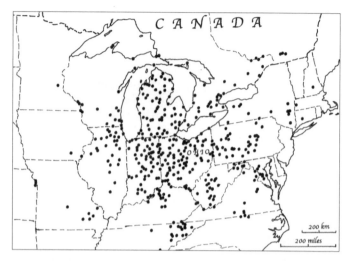

Fig. 75 Distribution of Emerald Ash Borer as reported in 2013. The spots are one per American county, and therefore underestimate the density of attack.

Presumably in its East Asian home it came to terms, over millions of years of evolution, with the local species of ash, as *Hylesinus* has done in Europe. In America, *Agrilus* meets unfamiliar, susceptible species of ash and escapes the predators of its homeland – within 11 years of arriving in an area, the beetle's population explodes and kills all the ash trees. Ash being one of the commonest remaining trees, the result is whole landscapes of dead ashes, especially in towns. The dead trees, too many for tree-fellers to get round to them, fall on cars and people's heads. Human health is affected as people are suddenly deprived of their favourite trees and exposed to high temperatures and air pollution.

Emerald Ash Borer was first noticed in 2002. The

authorities imposed quarantine, but to little effect. The nursery and firewood trades are said to have spread it to fresh areas; it has already killed more ashes than there are in the whole of Britain and Ireland. An industry has grown up for injecting or spraying ash trees with insecticide. This can probably save only a few specially significant trees, but gains time to work out a policy. Bee-keepers complain of insecticides getting into bees as they gather ash pollen. It is proposed to try biological control by introducing Chinese predators and parasites of the insect.

At the time of writing the beetle had jumped west to Kansas and east to New Hampshire (Fig. 75). It seems only a matter of time before it jumps the Atlantic. There are already reports that it has reached Moscow westward through Siberia. What happens when Emerald Ash Borer reaches Britain?

6 Recent past and future

Approximately half of ash saplings and young trees planted in the UK are imported. The annual value to UK importers of trading young ash trees is tentatively estimated at up to £300,000.

DEFRA, March 2013

The twentieth century was kind to ash

ASH HAS BEEN INCREASING throughout the Holocene. Widespread since wildwood times, it seems to have got slowly commoner as the centuries have passed. In Anglo-Saxon times it was common but not universal: the sort of tree that places could be named after. It has slowly increased ever since, both in woodland and elsewhere.

In many coppice-woods ancient ash stools are outnumbered by younger ashes that have been felled twice or once or not at all. Limestone ashwoods in the Mendips, Derbyshire and Shropshire seem to have been ash-dominated for little more than a century; alternative trees would be hazel, or less likely lime. Even in oakwoods, the latest generation of trees tends to be ash (Fig. 76). New ashwoods have arisen on abandoned land, especially since grey squirrels prevented hazel from being a competitor. The ex-industrial valleys of South Wales are verdant with ash trees, not there in 1930s photographs.

From 1950 to 1975 (the 'years that the locusts have eaten') ancient woods were dug up to make farmland; others were

Fig. 76 Twentieth-century spread: a dense stand of young ash trees has filled a gap in mainly oakwood. Powerstock Common, Dorset, 2011.

felled and poisoned and made into conifer plantations. Ash fared not too badly. It was moderately resistant to the then Forestry Commission's poisons. In many plantations the occasional ash stool remains as a relict of what was there before. Often, both planted and native trees died, and the site was taken over by a new generation of self-sown ashes. In Gamlingay Wood, Cambridgeshire, where various treatments were tried in the 1950s, by 1991 I found that surviving stools, planted trees and self-sown trees were no more abundant in areas where ash was planted than where other trees were planted.

The increase of ash is slowing because of exploding numbers of deer. If the present trees die from Ash Disease or Emerald Ash Borer, deer will prevent a new generation from arising to replace them.

Climate change

I write these words from a sickbed in middle Texas. The local woods contain an evergreen oak, deciduous oaks, a clonal elm (unravaged by Elm Disease), a hackberry (*Celtis*, related to elm), the mysterious bo'd'arc tree (*Maclura pomifera*), a big juniper, and many others. These are mostly smallish trees, as befits the dry climate; they grow on the limestone cliffs of canyons or on the deeper soils of canyon bottoms. Ash is represented by *Fraxinus texensis*, almost confined to Texas. This little tree grows on shallow soils or in rockholes, often with a lignotuberous base like a coppice stool.

This landscape is not unchanging. For most of the Holocene, Plains Indians and their Woodland Culture predecessors maintained the prairies and savannas between the canyons by burning to favour the buffalo and deer that they hunted. After a brief period of cowboys-and-Indians culture, European settlers came in the 1840s, began cultivating the savannas, and suppressed fire. This phase did not last and when abandoned resulted in a huge expansion of juniper. Neither fire, nor lack of fire, nor cultivation had much effect on the canyons, which were affected by woodcutting for about a century. The present situation is probably more wooded than at any time in the Holocene.

Fig. 77 *Fraxinus texensis* suffering from drought: this tree has so far escaped with bunched foliage, while thousands of others have died. Middle Texas, May 2013.

Here weather is more significant than climate. In 1992, the wettest season since Europeans came, rainfall filled the canyons with mighty rivers that left debris hanging high in the bottomland trees. In 2011 there was a huge drought, after which about one-eighth of the trees, including ashes, died (Fig. 77). Let us not, however, cry Climate Change. This was not the greatest drought even since Europeans came. In a semi-arid climate droughts and floods are part of the *normal dynamics* that sustain ecosystems. When a change in human affairs allows trees to increase they can be expected to arise in larger numbers than the climate will sustain: at the next big drought the less well-equipped individuals – often younger trees – fight for moisture with their neighbours, and lose.

How does this transfer to Britain? Here ash, like most other trees, is not near its geographical limit: it extends far south into lands that are already as warm as global warming is likely to make Britain. Ash with us is not particularly susceptible to climate change – unlike the special ash species of American mountain tops, trapped on 'sky islands' with nowhere to go if the climate turns against them.

That said, the great drought of 1975–6 was accompanied by severe ash dieback in the East Midlands. There were thousands of half-dead hedgerow ashes, whose remaining foliage was often bunched into clusters. (Could *Hymenoscyphus* have been involved?) It was reminiscent of the oak dieback reported after the great drought of 1919. Ash is resilient and survives decimation; the dead boughs have disappeared and been replaced by new leafage. Ash dieback was not repeated after the more recent droughts.

The future of ash

I dare not predict what will happen to ash; the recent cycle of Elm Disease is too uncomfortable a precedent. Who would have foreseen in 1970 that 40 years on the geographical distribution of the various elms would be almost unaltered, but *big* elms would still be abundant only in Huntingdonshire, Cambridgeshire woodland, east Sussex and the Isles of Scilly?

Of the influences on ash in Britain, climate change appears not to be significant. Deer will make ash less of a woodland tree. Coppicing of ash, already precarious because of deer damage, will be threatened because coppice shoots appear to attract *Chalara* (see Fig. 73, page 131).

Fig. 78 Not all dieback of ash is due to Ash Disease. This is probably drought. Kingcombe, Dorset, September 2012.

Ash Disease has been studied for at most 20 years, too little to establish the parameters of its behaviour in big versus small trees, old versus middle-aged, woodland versus non-woodland, fast- versus slow-growing, planted versus natural trees, soil and climate. Whether these questions will ever be answered depends on whether Emerald Ash Borer jumps the Atlantic and devours European ashes as it has devoured American.

What might replace ash? Hazel and oak no longer reproduce in existing woodland owing to introduced pests: grey squirrel for hazel, and for oak probably oak mildew. Birch is a likely replacement, considering how readily it replaced planted trees (of whatever species) in the twentieth century. Maple, hornbeam, hawthorn and (the often unwelcome) sycamore are alternatives. The future, however, is in the mouths of deer: aspen, being unpalatable, gains a competitive advantage.

Globalisation of pests and diseases

Plant diseases are not new. The ancient Romans sacrificed puppies to propitiate Robigo, the god or goddess of wheat rust.[1] Much earlier, the Elm Decline in the early Neolithic was apparently due to Dutch Elm Disease. Was this related to the beginnings of agriculture? Did Neolithic people introduce the disease? Did agriculture help it to spread? Conversely, did farmers spread into north Europe because a disease had cleared land for them? Did Elm Disease trigger the Neolithic Revolution?

For thousands of years people have been moving plants around the globe. In 1787 William Bligh of the *Bounty* was sent to Tahiti to collect breadfruit plants to take to the Caribbean to feed slaves, but something nasty happened to him and the plants were thrown overboard. Four years later he tried again – successfully, until the slaves refused to eat the breadfruit. On voyages round Cape Horn, any parasites would probably die out or kill their hosts on the way.

After 1833, live plants were taken more securely in Wardian cases (miniature greenhouses, Fig. 79). With steamships, globalisation went up a gear as parasites survived faster ocean

1 Columella, *De Re Rustica* 10: 337ff.

Fig. 79 Wardian case for intercontinental transport of live plants

crossings. Three American grape parasites – phylloxera, downy and powdery mildew – came in the nineteenth century, and many others in the early to mid-twentieth.

There were even deliberate introductions. In 1868–9, Monsieur Trouvelot, a French dissident living in Massachusetts, imported gypsy moths from Europe to teach them to be silkworms. He got no silk out of them, but let some escape: they got into the woods and now defoliate the trees on an 11-year cycle. The caterpillars are hated by foresters and gardeners, but they probably do less ecological damage than the succession of frantic and futile attempts that the authorities have made to 'control' them.

Globalisation goes into overdrive

Who remembers the 'Plant a Tree in '73' campaign? What happened to all the trees planted in 1973? How many are still alive 40 years on? I was suspicious at the time: was all that planting really necessary? Was it really a substitute for conserving native trees? As one forester, Richard Pawsey, said at the time:

> The present enthusiasm for tree-planting . . . masks an almost total ignorance of how to keep them alive.
>
> *New Scientist,* 22 November, 1973

Peter Sell, plant taxonomist, pointed out that what were sold as 'native' trees were often lookalikes from anywhere between here and Japan. Until recently, gardeners made it a point of honour not to grow native plants: bluebells in one's garden must not be the beautiful and romantic native bluebell, but Spanish Bluebell, which gets into native woods via garden throwouts and displaces the native bluebell. Tree-planting, like muntjac deer and grey squirrels, was another aspect of *Homo sapiens's* tendency to mix up all the world's plants and animals regardless of consequences.

Planting went industrial. It entered a world of grants and tenders and contracts and subcontracts and work to be finished on time and money to be spent before the financial year's end: an environment geared to the anthropology of bureaucrats and at odds with the 'real' world of trees and parasites. A subcontractor, required to produce so many oak seedlings and finding oaks did not bear acorns this season, goes to another country with more reliable acorns and cheaper labour: he brings in the oaks and any disease on them that is not too obtrusive. As if the depths of commercial frivolity had still not been plumbed, one hears of collecting seed in Britain, sending it to be germinated on the Continent, bringing back the

Fig. 80 Is all tree-planting good planting? A late-twentieth century 'broadleaf' plantation, mostly ash, with discarded plastic tree guards and many failed trees.

seedlings (and any disease they may have picked up), and selling them as of 'local provenance'!

Timber merchants' websites reveal the same 'coals-to-Newcastle' attitude. Although log prices for ash in Britain are at a historic low, much of the ash timber sold in Britain is brought from America, and some from the Continent. (And much of the ash timber grown in Britain is sent to the Continent.) This exchange would not have contributed to the coming of Ash Disease, which begins on leaves, but it could easily let in Emerald Ash Borer. No doubt the regulations impose precautions, but they are unlikely to be completely effective. The future of ash in Europe ought not to depend on an American inspector being willing to stay on an extra half-hour on a Friday afternoon to finish the job.

How much will be left in another hundred years?

About as many introduced tree diseases have appeared since the 1970s as in all the years before (*see* Table 4).

In 2003 I visited the State of Ohio, where my hosts took me into the field. I had not expected to see the American Chestnut:

> Under a spreading chestnut tree
> The village smithy stands
>
> Longfellow, *The Village Blacksmith* (1839)

The East Asian fungus *Endothia* (*Cryphonectria*) *parasitica* came early in the twentieth century, and *Castanea dentata,* the American Chestnut, is now rarer than the village smithy. Most elms had been subtracted by Dutch Elm Disease from Eurasia. Most red oaks had succumbed to Oak Wilt (Fig. 81), related to Dutch Elm Disease. Where was *Cornus florida*, the most beautiful American flowering shrub, the State Flower of Virginia? Lost to the new fungus *Discula destructiva*. On the border of the state, the European insect *Adelges piceæ* was sucking the local fir trees dry. This left ash as the commonest remaining tree in much of Ohio. The Federal Government had spent millions of dollars on keeping Emerald Ash Borer from crossing from Canada. I predicted that Uncle Sam would fail: he has since spent tens of millions and has failed. All this has been in less than a hundred years.

In 2010, I was in Kyoto, Japan, surrounded by richly

Fig. 81 Oak Wilt (*Ceratocystis fagacearum*). The tree, an Inland Live-oak, should be evergreen. Middle Texas, 1996.

wooded mountains. In the previous 12 months one-tenth of the trees had died, but not because anyone had failed to keep the Kyoto Protocol on Climate Change (Fig. 82). The pines, *Pinus densiflora* – a most important cultural and historic tree, related to Scots Pine – had succumbed to *Bursaphelenchus xylophilus*, an eelworm supposedly introduced from America in the 1930s. The commonest oak, *Quercus*

Table 4 Major introductions of plant diseases and insect pests

Condition	Agent	Vector	Source	Destination
pre-1800				
Elm Disease	*Ceratocystis ulmi*	fungus	?	Europe (*c.*4000 BC)
1845–1900 (steamships)				
Potato Blight	*Phytophthora infestans*	fungus	America	Skye & Ireland Europe
Vine Powdery Mildew	*Uncinula necator*	fungus	N. America	France, Europe
Vine Downy Mildew	*Plasmopara viticola*	fungus	N. America	France, Europe
Vine Phylloxera	*Daktulosphaira vitifolia*	aphid	N. America	France, Europe
Gypsy Moth	*Lymantria dispar*	moth	France	N. America
White Pine Blister Rust	*Cronartium ribicola*	fungus	Europe	N. America
1900–1950				
Oak Mildew	*Microsphæra alphitoides*	fungus	N. America	Europe
Pine Eelworm	*Bursaphelenchus xylophilus*	nematode	N. America	Japan
Chestnut Blight	*Endothia parasitica*	fungus	E. Asia	Europe
Chestnut Blight	*Endothia parasitica*	fungus	E. Asia	N. America
Elm Disease	*Ceratocystis sp.*	fungus	Europe	N. America
Cypress Disease	*Seiridium cardinale*	fungus	California	Europe
W. Australia Dieback	*Phytophthora cinnamomi*	water-mould	?	SW Australia
Oak Wilt	*Ceratocystis fagacearum*	fungus	?	N. America
1950–1975				
Fireblight (pears)	*Erwinia amylovora*	bacterium	N.America?	Europe
Fir Adelgid	*Adelges piceae*	insect	Europe	N. America
Hemlock Adelgid	*Adelges tsugae*	insect	E. Asia	N. America
Knopper Gall (oak)	*Andricus quercuscalicis*	gall-wasp	S. Europe	England
Horsechestnut Bleed	*Phytophthora sp.*	water-mould	?	Britain
Elm Disease	*Ceratocystis novo-ulmi*	fungus	N. America	Europe
Elm Leaf Beetle	*Xanthogaleruca luteola*	insect	S. Europe	N. America

Condition	Agent	Vector	Source	Destination
1975–2000				
Horsechestnut Bleed	*Pseudomonas syringae*	bacterium	?	Europe
Dogwood Anthracnose	*Discula destructiva*	fungus	?	N. America
Red-band Needle-blight (pine)	*Dothistroma septosporum*	fungus	?	worldwide
Box Blight	*Cylindrocladium buxicola*	fungus	?	Europe
Alder Disease	*Phytophthora alni*	water-mould	?	England
Pine Adelgid	*Marchalina hellenica*	insect	?	Greece
Konara Oak Disease	*Raffaelea quercivora*	fungus + insect vector	?	Japan
Acute Oak Decline	?	bacterium?	?	England
Red Palm Weevil	*Rhynchophorus ferrugineus*	insect	S. Asia	Mediterranean, Middle East
Sudden Oak Death	*Phytophthora ramorum*	water-mould	?	California, Britain
2000–2013				
Sudden Oak Death (variant)	*Phytophthora kernoviæ*	water-mould	?	Britain, Ireland
Horsechestnut Leaf-miner	*Cameraria ohridella*	micro-moth	Balkans	Europe
Emerald Ash Borer	*Agrilus planipennis*	beetle	E. Asia	N. America
Elm Leaf Beetle	*Xanthogaleruca luteola*	insect	S. Europe	Tasmania*
Ash Disease	*Chalara fraxinea*	fungus	East?	Europe
Plane Disease	*Ceratocystis platani*	fungus	?	France, Greece

* Elms were introduced from Britain to Tasmania and are now an important tree; they are remote enough to have escaped Elm Disease, but are threatened by this beetle.

Fig. 82 Omen of things to come? On the mountains around Kyoto, Japan, about one-tenth of the trees died in the year 2010. The *konara* oak, *Quercus serrata*, was killed by a combination of a fungus and its insect vector. The *akamatsu* pine, *Pinus densiflora*, was killed by an American eelworm.

Fig. 83 One of the great ecological tragedies of the last century: the introduction of a common tropical soil *Phytophthora* to the unique ecosystems of south-west Australia. Dead jarrah eucalyptus and many other plants. December 1996.

serrata, was killed by a combination of the fungus *Raffaelea quercivora* and its insect vector *Platypus quercivorus* (not to be confused with its Australian namesake). (On the dead oaks was also the spectacular fungus, *Podostroma cornu-damae*, which I was warned was poisonous to taste, touch and smell.) The second preferred host was *Quercus mongolica*, the nearest equivalent to English oak.

One of the great ecological tragedies of the twentieth century was in south-west Australia, with hundreds of peculiar and bizarre plant species confined for millions of years to a small area between the sea and the desert. Someone let in *Phytophthora 'cinnamomei'*, a fungus-like water-mould that is a minor tropical pathogen, widespread everywhere else. The special plants, including jarrah, *Eucalyptus marginata*, one of the world's biggest trees, were disastrously susceptible and have been succumbing ever since (Fig. 83).

In Crete, pine trees are attacked by the insect *Marchalina hellenica*, which looks like a woolly aphid and tells a bizarre story of human folly. You, gentle reader, probably think Greek honey is made from the nectar of thyme and other flowers. Much of it originates in the sugary honeydew that bees collect from the back ends of insects that feed on trees. There was nothing wrong with tree honey until beekeepers were encouraged, indeed subsidised, to spread *Marchalina* as a source of honeydew. Too late it was found that the pine trees die.

Cypress trees in Britain and Crete, as all over Europe, are killed by the fungus *Seiridium cardinale*, globalised from California. By great good fortune it affects the garden form of cypress, shaped like a Lombardy Poplar, but not the wild cypress, that majestic and defining tree of the Cretan mountains.

As if this were not enough, Crete, like many other countries, has been given the Red Palm Weevil, a giant insect that burrows into and kills palm trees. Palms are fashionable trees to import, and the weevil comes with them. It threatens the native Cretan palm, one of the world's rarest and most romantic trees (Fig. 84). The moral of this is: (1) planted trees can threaten existing trees of the same or related species; (2) an industry has grown up for 'treating' infected trees and disposing of dead trees, and there are people whose livelihood depends on never getting rid of the insect.

Britain has been let off comparatively lightly

Oak Mildew, previously an American fungus, appeared throughout Europe in about 1908. Everyone now knows the white film that covers oak leaves in mid and late summer (Fig. 85). It may seem trivial, but around this time oak suddenly and permanently changed its ecology. Having previously grown well from seed in existing woods, it changed to being light-demanding, oak seedlings growing almost everywhere *except* in a wood: was this because they could cope with shade or mildew, but not both together?

Dutch Elm Disease, which had flared up in the eighteenth and nineteenth centuries, did so again in the 1920s, and again in the 1970s. In the 1920s it had been taken on elm bark to America, where it destroyed millions of elms and in the process underwent a genetic change which made it even more aggressive when it was taken back on elm bark to Europe *c.* 1970 (Fig. 88).

Fig. 84 The genuine palm tree of Europe at Préveli, Crete, June 2011. *Phœnix theophrasti* is a relict from the Tertiary geological period, 6 million years ago, now one of the world's rarest trees. The palms are not threatened by fire, which they are well adapted to. They are threatened because fools have been importing exotic palm trees to Crete, and with them the Red Palm Weevil, a worldwide threat to cultivated palms (*below right*) and wild palms. An industry has arisen of 'treating' weevil-infested palm trees, as in Cyprus (*below left*).

Fig. 85 Oak Mildew (*Microsphæra alphitoides*) introduced from North America *c.*1900. Middlemarsh, Dorset, September 2002.

Fig. 86 Sudden Oak Death (*Phytophthora ramorum*), a fungus of unknown origin, was first noticed in California where it attacks oak-like trees (whence the name). In 2002 it was noticed in Britain, where it attacks rhododendron and larch (not native oaks). It has rapidly spread and is taking out most of the plantations of larch, one of the few otherwise successful forestry conifers. Wentwood, Monmouthshire, September 2013.

Fig. 87 Black bleeding from an oak, associated with the still mysterious Acute Oak Decline. Madingley Wood, Cambridge, 2004.

The Forestry Commission has stopped planting Corsican Pine because of Red-Band Needle-Blight. This affects many pines and threatens worldwide cellulose supplies, as it attacks *Pinus radiata*, said to be the world's most abundantly planted timber tree.

Britain has acquired new *Phytophthoras*: one has been eating up alder since the 1990s; others have attacked horsechestnuts and other trees since the 1970s. Another *Phytophthora* is responsible for 'Sudden Oak Death', as California called it. In Britain it began to attack not oak but exotic rhododendrons, then turned its attention to larch, and is proceeding to take out all larch forestry plantations (Fig. 86).

Oak is menaced by Acute Oak Decline, apparently a bacterial condition (Fig. 87); and by the unexplained expansion of *Agrilus planipennis* (*biguttatus*), a bark beetle that

Fig. 88 Elm Disease globalised into America (Williamstown, Massachusetts, 1981, *left*), and was then brought back to its Old World origin (*above*, 1978).

makes D-shaped holes in the trunks of weakly oaks, which ten years ago was an insect of Red Data Book rarity.

Since 2008, nearly all horsechestnuts in Europe have been attacked by a microscopic caterpillar, *Cameraria ohridella*. This eats out the chlorophyll-bearing middle of the leaf thickness (Fig. 90). Horsechestnut itself is an exotic, introduced some 400 years ago, ultimately from its glacial refuge in a small area of the Balkans around Ohrid, where it is a small tree confined to cliffs (Fig. 89). It looks as though a predator, originally from that area (whence the name), has at last caught up with the host tree. As befits a natural predator, it does not hurt the tree much.

Can trade kill trees?

Globalisation of diseases has become the top threat to the world's trees and forests. Exotic diseases subtract 'keystone' species one by one from ecosystems, sometimes almost overnight, more efficiently than deer and much more efficiently than climate change. People are being urged to plant trees to store carbon dioxide. Why bother, if they succumb to disease, rot, and let the CO_2 back into the atmosphere?

Intercontinental trade takes pests and diseases which had come to terms with their hosts through co-adaptation over millions of years, and introduces them to new, unadapted hosts. There is also the prospect, especially with *Phytophthoras*, that separated pathogenic species are brought together and hybridise to create new and aggressive pathogens.

There is an analogy with bees. Reader, you may think the humble bumblebee is indigenous, bumbling away to

Fig. 89 Horsechestnut originated from a small part of the Balkans, around the city of Ohrid, and in the wild is a small tree confined to cliffs. It was introduced to western Europe four centuries ago. Vikos Gorge, northern Greece, 2009.

Fig. 90 The leaf-mining micro-moth, *Cameraria ohridella*, apparently comes, like the horsechestnut, from around the city of Ohrid.

provide what scholastic writers call 'ecosystem services' for the human lords of creation, like a labourer earning the National Minimum Wage. In reality, she is imported from God knows where to pollinate tomato and strawberry crops. The volume of trade in bumblebees defeats the regulations that are supposed to keep out diseases, some of which affect hive-bees too. A recent investigation reports that most of the officially 'parasite-free' imported colonies carry parasites.[2] This never-ending import of parasites appears to be a factor in the general decline of bees in Britain.

Can't introduced tree diseases be controlled?

In the nineteenth century the three American vine diseases came within an inch of abolishing wine, anticipating the American Prohibitionists. Wine-growing survived, but in a permanently more complex and expensive form: grafting and chemical spraying are necessary to get a crop at all. Plant diseases affecting crops are dealt with by a combination of chemicals and plant breeding, neither of which works well with trees, especially wild trees. English Elm was a supertree, cloned by people for centuries – until it proved super-susceptible to the 1970s strain of Elm Disease.

Concerning Ash Disease, a report by the Department for Environment, Food and Rural Affairs (DEFRA) in 2013 proposes 'developing resistance to the disease in the ash population'. This is not quite as absurd as it seems. Although plants do not have the immune system that enables

2 P Graystock et al. 2013 'The Trojan hives: pollinator pathogens, imported and distributed in bumblebee colonies' *Journal of Applied Ecology* 50 1207–15.

vertebrate animals to acquire resistance to foot-and-mouth or leprosy, ash's damage-limitation mechanism determines how far a *Chalara* infection progresses in the tree. However, to suggest that a Ministry, or any other human institution, can influence this process is a vain aspiration. (If it can be done, why haven't East Europeans done it ten years ago?) Trees have a generation time of tens or hundreds of years: pathogens can run rings round them in evolutionary terms. The government, in its ill-informed optimism, expects the present ash trees somehow to be replaced by a new generation that is resistant to *Chalara*. Even if deer hold off, long before that happens the Emerald Ash Borer will have arrived and eaten whatever ash trees survive *Chalara*.

There is only half an instance in Europe of a disease of wild trees being controlled, let alone exterminated. Chestnut blight almost destroyed the chestnut trees (*Castanea sativa*) which had been a major food source in southern Europe. In the 1960s it ceased to be a problem, not because anyone did anything, but because God raised up a fungal virus which crippled the fungus and made it incapable of damaging the tree. The Apennines are full of huge trees that once were five-sixths dead (Fig. 91). On Mount Athos, the Holy Mountain in north Greece, the monasteries depend for their livelihood on coppiced chestnut woods, an isolated population of chestnut only recently reached by the disease. In 2001, the monks (who are keen on technology) were busy inoculating their trees with virus-infected fungus. This is half an instance, because all attempts to get the virus going in North America have failed.

Fig. 91 Chestnut blight, introduced in the 1920s. These veteran trees have recovered because of the appearance of a fungal virus, leaving huge dead trunks. Liguria, Italy, 1984.

Reaction of the authorities

The authorities have not been inactive. Travellers, bringing back little Christmas trees in their luggage, are persecuted by the Customs – in theory. Since 1993, plant passports have allowed registered growers to move live plants within the European Union. Maybe this keeps out known and conspicuous pests like the big jolly Colorado Beetle. Plant passports are unlikely to work for unknown and inconspicuous diseases. They did not keep out Ash Disease.

I used to say that any of the world's plant diseases can enter Britain provided it does so via some other European Union country. (Ash Disease has done just that.) By the time the problem has been detected and the bureaucracy has clanked into action, it is too late. Imports of ash trees should have been banned in the 1990s, as soon as Ash Disease was detected in Europe.

At a conference in Ireland in 2004, I remarked that the Irish had had enough experience of imported plant disease to last them a thousand years – the calamitous potato famine in 1845. The man from the Ministry got up and bleated that nothing could be done because this would restrict trade and the World Trade Organization would not allow it. Either the WTO or the European Union will not let the stable door be locked until plant pathologists have certified that the horse has gone: as has just happened, yet again, with Ash Disease.

My first reaction to the Forestry Commission survey was amazement and dismay that people should have been planting ash in several hundred sites. If people have planted ash in hundreds of locations, something is wrong with the human culture. Numbers of ashlings imported, before *Chalara* struck, are variously estimated at between 1½ and 3½ million a year, mainly from Germany and the Netherlands. Ash is very common and is getting commoner: why plant it on this scale?

DEFRA produced a lengthy report on Ash Disease making much of the meagre evidence. Their 'science-based' advice amounts to: Do Nothing. For once I agree: this time they are being realistic with a disease that is inconspicuous, ill-defined, and affects a very common tree. Even finding out who owns the ash trees in Britain is an almost superhuman task.

Some talk of 'eliminating' the disease by sanitation felling. This might have worked 15 years ago when it was rare, but is too late now. There is no point in not moving logs, for this is not how Ash Disease gets about (unlike Emerald Ash Borer). The public has been told to 'wash your boots and wash the dog and wash the children' after visiting a wood. This might work if you washed the deer too. Like the ancient Romans, why not try sacrificing puppies?

Some talk of fungicide sprays: this would involve soaking whole landscapes in fungicide year after year until *Chalara* responded by evolving resistance. It might favour *Chalara* by damaging other fungi antagonistic to it. At best a fungicide might work for saving individual, specially significant trees.

DEFRA produced 34 pages of verbiage on *Chalara*, the No.2 threat to ash trees that has got here and is uncontrollable, without one mention of Emerald Ash Borer, the No.1 threat, that could yet be kept out.

The government has thrown a modest amount of money at the disease, by instituting a research programme. Good – but other countries have already gone much further. However, such researches still treat Ash Disease in isolation.

A Greek forester recently introduced me to *Ceratocystis platani*, a new and mortal disease of plane, which in Greece is probably the third-commonest wild tree and of immense cultural importance. This plane equivalent of Dutch Elm Disease has also got into the south of France. Do people import plane trees to Britain? Are they allowed to?

What can be done?

> You can't provide in advance for unknown contingencies.
> In practice, your special precautions degenerate into mere
> formalities.

> R.A. Freeman, 'The Contents of a Mare's Nest' (1927)

1. Recognise the problem. Whether or not Ash Disease turns out to be quite as bad as was anticipated in 2012, it is not an isolated problem. Tree disease has struck half-a-dozen times, and each time is still treated as happenstance, rather than as part of a wider pattern, as enemy action. Governments throw a little money at each separate disease after it has arrived. They are ill-suited to deal with the wider problem, because each government encounters only one new tree disease; when the next disease arrives it will be a new government which will treat it as a new problem and will not learn from last time or look forward to next time. The public, faced with a depleting landscape, regards depletion as normal. Since the last Elm Disease a new generation has grown up to accept the absence of big elms as normal – even ecologists fail to notice or study places where big elms survive or are returning.

2. As John Gibbs, the great tree pathologist, has pointed out, it is no good reacting to known plant diseases: that battle has already been fought and mostly lost. What is needed is to forestall diseases that have not yet got here or are still unknown. For ash trees, the latest year in which to react to *Chalara* was 1995. The real threat is now not *Chalara* but the Emerald Ash Borer.

Fig. 92 Make use of being an island. The Isles of Scilly pictured in May 2012. Far out in the Atlantic, the islands escaped the 1970s Elm Disease and still have a full complement of elms. Will the Outer Hebrides be the last refuge of ash?

3. Don't use climate change as a let-out for inaction. If global warming were the underlying cause, then each hot summer would see tree diseases from the south extending their range northward. That is not the pattern: unknown diseases suddenly appear, usually from west to east or east to west, regardless of weather or climate.

4. Make use of being an island. The Isles of Scilly out in the Atlantic still have a full complement of great elms (Fig. 92). Banning imports before the event might not have kept Ash Disease out of Britain, but probably would have kept it out of Ireland. Chile is, in effect, an island, isolated by the ocean, the Andes, and the Atacama Desert, and (I am told) is determined to remain so: it stringently forbids commercial imports of plants and soil, especially in order to protect its pre-phylloxera grapevines.

5. Get real. Stop letting the anthropology of commerce overrule the practical world. Stop treating plants (and bees) as mere articles of trade, like cars or tins of paint, to be made and brought in industrial quantities from anywhere. Importing a million cars does not imperil the cars that are already here, but trees are different. Nobody *has* to import trees commercially: it is only an artefact of how business happens to be conducted. What matters is *volume*. My little Christmas tree from an Alpine holiday will not do much harm. But a commercial supplier, importing a million container-grown hawthorns from Ruritania (as though there were no hawthorns in Britain!), inevitably imports a thousand tons of Ruritanian soil and whatever is in it. However thoroughly the Customs, or a responsible nurseryman, inspect the consignment, they cannot detect a microscopic pathogen when they do not know in advance what to look for. If it is ash trees, imported in winter, they will not detect all *Chalara* even if they do know what to look for. Trees should be imported only in small numbers for special reasons, with precautions that are impractical with commercial shipments.

6. Plant fewer trees, more expensive trees, wider apart, and take proper care of them. Stop making tree-planting a default option, as in the Scots proverb: 'Ye may be aye stickin' in a tree; it'll be growin' while ye're sleepin'. This casual mindset needs to be changed. It would be disastrous if the death of ashes were made the pretext for a massive replanting, bringing in more foreign stock and more foreign diseases. The pros and cons of every planting need to be formally assessed, including the risk that planting trees will kill existing trees. Tree-planting, like chemicals, is not risk-free: if not used sparingly it will lose its effectiveness.

7. Revive the science of tree pathology. Although the underlying problem belongs to anthropology rather than science, the understanding of tree diseases has been scandalously neglected in Britain. (I except the recent revival at Bangor University.) I was taught tree diseases in Cambridge Botany School by Denis Garrett and John Rishbeth. I read research papers and passed examinations; although my career has been in other directions I have maintained a lifelong interest. Times have changed. Garrett and Rishbeth retired, Cambridge University failed to replace them, and their expertise was lost. My contemporary was John Gibbs OBE, who became head of the Forestry Commission's pathology department and retired in 2001. Botany turned into Plant Sciences, of which tree pathology was not one. I understand there are about a dozen of us left in Britain. I am one of the last survivors of a Critically Endangered Species. I belong in the Zoo.

Bibliography

GENERAL

Loudon, J.C. (1838) *Arboretum et Fruticetum Britannicum*

Peterken, G.F. (2013) 'Ash – an ecological portrait' *British Wildlife* 24 235–42

Rackham, O. (1975) *Hayley Wood: its history and ecology,* Cambridgeshire & Isle of Ely Naturalists' Trust

Rackham, O. (1986) *The History of the Countryside,* Dent

Rackham, O. (1980) *Ancient Woodland: its history, vegetation and uses in England,* Edward Arnold (2nd ed Castlepoint Press 2003)

Rackham, O. (2006) *Woodlands* (New Naturalist), Harper Collins

Rackham, O. (2008) 'Ancient woodlands: modern threats' (Tansley Review) *New Phytologist* 180 571–86

Vera, F.W.M. (2000) *Grazing Ecology and Forest History* CABI, Wallingford

Wardle, P. (1961) 'Biological Flora of the British Isles: *Fraxinus excelsior L.*' *Journal of Ecology* 49 739–51

THE ASH TREE

Austin, P. (2013) 'Pollards in early-modern South East Hertfordshire' *The Local Historian* 43 138–58

Blackstock, T.H. (2013) 'Synchronised variation in fruit production in *Fraxinus excelsior*' B[otanical] S[ociety of the] B[ritish] I[sles] News 123 15–6

Bosanquet, S. (2013) 'Ash and its host species: bryophytes' *British Wildlife* 24 247–50

Edwards, B. (2013) 'Ash and its host species: lichens' *British Wildlife* 24 243–6

Elwes, H.J. & Henry, A. (1906) *The Trees of Great Britain and Ireland,* Edinburgh

Peterken, G.F. (1976) 'Long-term changes in the woodlands of Rockingham Forest and other areas' *Journal of Ecology* 64 123–46

Peterken, G.F. (1981) *Woodland Conservation and Management,* Chapman & Hall

Synge, A.D. (1947) 'Pollen collection by honeybees (*Apis mellifera*)' *Journal of Animal Ecology* 16 122–38

Tansley, A.G. (1936) *The British Islands and their Vegetation,* Cambridge University Press

PREHISTORY AND HISTORY

Davenport, F.G. (1906) *The Economic Development of a Norfolk Manor* [Forncett] *1086–1565,* Cambridge

Peglar, S. (1990) 'The mid-Holocene Ulmus decline at Diss Mere . . . a year-by-year pollen stratigraphy from annual laminations' *The Holocene* 3 1–13

Pryor, F. (2005) *Flag Fen: life and death of a prehistoric landscape,* History Press

Smith, L.D.W. (1981) 'A survey of building timber and other trees in the hedgerows of a Warwickshire estate, *c.*1500' *Transactions of the Birmingham & Warwickshire Archaeological Society* 90 65–73

Spriggs, J.A. (2002) 'Evidence for wood conversion and use' *Medieval Urbanism in Coppergate*, Council for British Archaeology 838–50

Stenning, D.F. (2003) 'Small aisled halls in Essex' *Vernacular Architecture* 34 1–19

VETERAN AND ANCIENT TREES

Elwes, H.J. and Henry A. (1900–1913) *The Trees of Great Britain and Ireland*

Shigo, A.L. (1983) *Tree Defects: a photo guide,* Forest Service, United States Department of Agriculture, Washington

Strutt, J.G. (1822) *Sylva Britannica*, Valpy, London

CULTURAL, SPIRITUAL AND MATERIAL

Anon. (1853) *English Forests and Forest Trees: historical, legendary, and descriptive*, Ingram Cooke, London

Bowett, A. (2012) *Woods in British furniture-making 1400–1900* Oblong, Wetherby

Edlin, H.L. (1949) *Woodland Crafts in Britain,* Batsford

Fitzrandolph, H.E. and Hay, M.D. (1926) *Timber and Underwood Industries and some Village Workshops,* Oxford

Hooke, D. (2010) *Trees in Anglo-Saxon England*, Boydell & Brewer

Hutton, R. (1991) *The Pagan Religions of the Ancient British Isles*, Wiley-Blackwell

Joyce, P.W. (1875) *Irish Names of Places,* 4th ed Dublin (I am indebted to Professor Fergus Kelly for this reference).

Lane, J. (1996) *John Hall and his Patients*, Shakespeare Birthplace Trust

Lucas, A.T. (1962) 'The sacred trees of Ireland' *Journal of Cork Historical & Archaeological Society* 68 40–54

Lynton, N. (2007) *David Nash*, Thames & Hudson

Mabey, R. (1998) *Flora Britannica,* Chatto & Windus

Reschreiter, H., Winner, G., Grabner, M., (2013) 'Esche einmal anders' *Dendro-Ecologie, Typologie,* Ökologie Festschrift für André Billamboz Janus-Verlag, Freiburg im Breisgau 139–44. (I am grateful to Dr Tomasz Wazny for bringing this to my attention).

Salzman, L.F. (1967) *Building in England Down to 1540,* Clarendon, Oxford 2nd ed

Vickery, R. (1995) *A Dictionary of Plant-Lore,* Oxford

PESTS AND DISEASES

Cooke, A.S. and Farrell, L. (2001) 'Impact of muntjac deer . . . at Monks Wood National Nature Reserve . . .' *Forestry* 74 241–9

Dennis, R.W.G. (1960) *British Cup Fungi and their Allies*, Ray Society, London

Elton, C.S. (1966) *The Pattern of Animal Communities,* Chapman & Hall, London

Jankovsky, L. and Holdenrieder, O. (2009) '*Chalara fraxinea* – Ash Dieback in the Czech Republic' *Plant Protection Science* 45 74–78

Patouillard, N.T. (1883–6) *Tabulæ Analyticæ Fungorum,* Klingsieck, Paris

Roberge, J.M. et al (2011) 'Edge creation and tree dieback influence the patch-tracking metapopulation dynamics of a red-listed epiphytic bryophyte' *Journal of Applied Ecology* 48 650–8

Queloz, V. et al (2011) 'Cryptic speciation in Hymenoscyphus albidus' *Forest Pathology* 41 133–42

RECENT PAST AND FUTURE

Chatters, C. (2013) 'Is tree-planting good for wildlife?' *British Wildlife* 24 162–6

Graystock, P. et al (2013) 'The Trojan hives: pollinator pathogens, imported and distributed in bumblebee colonies' *Journal of Applied Ecology* 50 1207–15

Worrell, R. (2013) *An Assessment of the Potential Impacts of Ash Dieback in Scotland*, www.forestry.gov.uk

Index and Glossary

Little Toller **Monographs**

Our monograph series is dedicated to new writing attuned to the natural world and which celebrates the rich variety of the places we live in. We have asked a wide range of the very best writers and artists to choose a particular building, plant, animal, myth, person or landscape, and through this object of their fascination tell us wider stories about the British Isles.

The first three titles

THE ASH TREE *Oliver Rackham*

HERBACEOUS *Paul Evans*

ON SILBURY HILL *Adam Thorpe*

In preparation

MERMAIDS *Sophia Kingshill*

LOST HOUSES *Ed Kluz*

FEN WALL *Richard Skelton*

RAIN *Melissa Harrison*

GOWER *Iain Sinclair*

LANDFILL *Tim Dee*

PEBBLES *Christopher Stocks & Angie Lewin*

A postcard sent to Little Toller will ensure you are put on our mailing list and amongst the first to discover each new book as it appears in the series. You can also follow our latest news at **littletoller.co.uk** or visit our online magazine **theclearingonline.org** for new essays, short films and poetry.

LITTLE TOLLER BOOKS

Lower Dairy, Toller Fratrum, Dorset DT2 0EL